D1649278

The Hidden Factor:
Why Thinking Differently Is
Your Greatest Asset

Scott E. Page, Ph.D.

THE
GREAT
COURSES

PUBLISHED BY:

THE GREAT COURSES
Corporate Headquarters
4840 Westfields Boulevard, Suite 500
Chantilly, Virginia 20151-2299
Phone: 1-800-832-2412
Fax: 703-378-3819
www.thegreatcourses.com

Scott E. Page, Ph.D.

Leonid Hurwicz Collegiate Professor
of Complex Systems, Political Science,
and Economics
University of Michigan

Professor Scott E. Page received a B.A. in Mathematics from the University of Michigan and an M.A. in Mathematics from the University of Wisconsin–Madison. He then received his M.S. in Business and his Ph.D. in Managerial Economics and Decision Sciences from the Kellogg School of Management at Northwestern University. He completed his Ph.D. thesis under the guidance of Stan Reiter and Nobel laureate Roger Myerson. He has been a Professor of Economics at the California Institute of Technology and The University of Iowa and is currently Leonid Hurwicz Collegiate Professor of Complex Systems, Political Science, and Economics at the University of Michigan. At Michigan, he is also a Senior Research Scientist at the Institute for Social Research, a Senior Fellow in the Society of Fellows, and the Director of the Center for the Study of Complex Systems. In addition, Professor Page has been a long-time External Professor for the Santa Fe Institute, an interdisciplinary think tank devoted to the study of complexity. In 2011, he was elected to the American Academy of Arts and Sciences.

Professor Page has won outstanding teaching assistant awards at the University of Wisconsin–Madison and Northwestern University, the Faculty Teaching Award at Caltech, and the Faculty Achievement Award for outstanding research, teaching, and service at the University of Michigan.

Professor Page's research interests span a wide range of disciplines. He has published more than 60 papers in a variety of fields, including economics, political science, computer science, physics, geography, public health, business, philosophy, and complexity. In addition, he has served on dissertation committees for students in more than 10 departments. In recent years, his core interest has been the various roles of diversity in complex adaptive systems, such as economies and ecosystems. His most recent book, *Diversity and Complexity*, explores the contributions of diversity to performance within complex systems. He is also the author of *Complex Adaptive Systems: An Introduction to Computational Models of Social Life* (with John H. Miller) and *The Difference: How the Power of Diversity Creates Better Groups, Firms, Schools, and Societies*. All three books were published by Princeton University Press.

A popular speaker, Professor Page has appeared at the Aspen Ideas Festival and the World Economic Forum and before numerous corporate and nonprofit audiences around the world, including Google, Ford, Genentech, the International Monetary Fund, and the Association of American Medical Colleges. He has also recorded *Understanding Complexity* with The Great Courses.

Professor Page lives with his wife and two sons in Ann Arbor, Michigan. ■

Table of Contents

Table of Contents

Table of Contents

The Hidden Factor:
Why Thinking Differently Is Your Greatest Asset

Scope:

In this course, you will explore the pragmatic benefits of diversity. You will see how differences in how people think contribute to collective performance in a variety of contexts—including how differences improve prediction and problem solving and how they make systems more robust.

The ideas in this course have the potential to transform how you think, live, and work and how people contribute to success in any group—from classrooms to whole societies. You will discover that your potential to contribute depends on building tools that complement the skills of others, and you will find that a focus on individual achievement can be self-defeating.

Optimal teams, groups, and societies require diverse talent, and in order to perform well, they must promote diverse ways of thinking. Diversity is linked to innovation and economic growth because continued growth depends on new perspectives and on recombining new ideas. Civilizations that do not promote diversity fail. As Jared Diamond shows in his paradigm-shifting book, *Collapse: How Societies Choose to Fail or Succeed*, an unwillingness to challenge status-quo thinking can be fatal.

In this course, you will learn how the lessons and insights of diversity have become even more relevant in an increasingly flat, complex world in which challenges and opportunities change quickly. In complex worlds, long-term success requires continued growth and the addition of new tools. Furthermore, you will learn about the no free lunch theorem, which implies that rules that have worked in the past will not necessarily work in the future. This insight can explain why the companies that were highlighted and touted by Jim Collins in *Good to Great: Why Some Companies Make the Leap ... and Others Don't* were mediocre performers in the decade following the book's publication.

It is through the demonstration of simple mathematics and logic that this course transforms metaphors about successful practices into scientific understandings. You will learn how cognitive difference plus cognitive depth allows groups to make better forecasts, find more innovative solutions to problems, and adapt to challenges. In addition, you will explore several core theoretical results. As a result of the diversity prediction theorem, you will discover that the ability of a crowd to make accurate predictions depends equally on their ability and their diversity. Through the application of the diversity trumps ability theorem, you will see how diversity can matter even more than ability in problem-solving contexts. More generally, you will learn that many types of diversity produce nearly inescapable benefits; however, not all types of diversity are beneficial. This course also covers the myriad problems created by preference diversity—differences in what people desire.

In this course, you will encounter topics such as groupthink and crowdsourcing, and you will learn how to make sound predictions using a variety of methods. This course will forever change how you think of diversity: You will no longer think of diversity in political or identity terms; instead, you will see diversity as central to understanding, progress, and robustness.

This course will share with you the theoretical and empirical evidence that underpin success and will offer practical lessons to improve how you think about the strategic makeup of any group. ∎

Individual Diversity and Collective Performance
Lecture 1

In this course, you are going to learn about diversity and innovation—about how individuals and collectives, as teams, use various methods to try to find novel solutions to problems. Along the way, you are going to learn about prediction, problem solving, innovation, economic growth, robustness, adaptation, and even groupthink. The goals of this lecture are to convince you of the importance of diversity, to describe the types of diversity that will be covered in this course, to give you some understanding of the causes of diversity, and to get you interested in and excited about the subject of diversity.

The Power of Diversity

- The idea that combinations of things can be more amazing than the things themselves holds true for neurons, for Legos, and even for people. Teams of people can accomplish things that no individual could do alone.

- Teams of people put men on the Moon. No one person could have done that. Not only was the set of problems required for space flight and lunar landings too large for any one person to solve them all, but it is also the case that many of these problems require teams of people to crack them. This is also true for the problems involved in creating the atomic bomb at Los Alamos, cracking the enigma code at Bletchley Park, and developing the technology required for telecommunication at Bell Laboratories.

- As the problems and challenges we face become more difficult and more **complex**, the value of **diversity** and teamwork becomes even greater. The first 15 Nobel Prizes in Physics went to a total of 19 people. The next 8 went to 8 people, and these included famous scientists such as Plank, Bohr, and Einstein. The last 15 Nobel prizes have been allocated among 42 people. This is a remarkable number—given the fact that at most 3 people can win. Furthermore, in almost every recent prize, several people were left out.

- Across scientific journals, the number of authors per paper has steadily increased over the past 30 years. More is better—not just because the task of writing a paper suddenly became bigger so that more heads are needed, but also because scientists have figured out that diverse teams are more productive. It's not that we lack great thinkers; teams are just better at solving scientific problems.

- At an individual level and as collectives—teams, groups, and whole societies—we benefit from different ways of thinking. At the same time, when other people talk about diversity, the subject often becomes politicized. This politicization and the contrast with what researchers have found showing the benefits of diversity in the scientific realm is the motivation for this course: to think about how diversity contributes to performance. Together, let's move this topic out of the political realm and think about diversity as scientists so that we can better solve problems and meet challenges.

© Digital Vision/Thinkstock.com.

The power of diversity is used in many areas—from the business world to the sciences. More and more work is based on group members contributing their diverse ideas to a problem in order to solve it.

- In the realm of business, more and more work is group based, and more and more workplaces are moving away from individual offices to shared offices and bullpens with open floor plans. In the Alcoa building in Pittsburgh, there are central escalators, and no one really has an office. Instead, there are cubicles everywhere.

- The benefits of diversity reach far beyond people interacting at larger scales within a single company. In his book *Triumph of the City*, Harvard economist Edward Glaeser provides a detailed account of how city workers—by being in contact with more diverse sets of ideas—are more productive than those that do not work in a city. In fact, Geoffrey West at the Santa Fe Institute has shown that worker productivity increases as city sizes increase.

- However, it is not the size that matters; instead, the diverse connections and interactions among people is what matters. Researchers Michael Macy, Nathan Eagle, and Rob Claxton were able to take phone data from England and reconstruct social networks. They found that diversity of calls correlates strongly with economic development at the city level. Surprisingly, the number of calls did not matter. For example, Stoke on Trent, which is a struggling area, had a higher-than-average call volume but had very low call diversity; in other words, they were calling the same people back and forth. However, Stratford on Avon, which is an affluent area, had an average call volume, but people tended to call diverse people.

- The fact that technology is bringing us all closer together means that we have the potential to tap into greater diversity. We can interact with people on projects from all over the world—even from different disciplines—at the same time in ways that would have been impossible a few decades ago. When we tap into that diversity, we can perform better.

The Benefits of Diversity

- When most people talk about diversity, they are referring to differences in how we look and where we come from—including race, gender, and ethnicity—which is called identity diversity. However, throughout this course, when we talk about diversity, we are referring to **cognitive diversity**, or differences in how we think—including **perspectives**, or the ways in which we encode problems; **heuristics**, or the tools and tricks we use to solve problems; **categories**, or the ways in which we parse the world into piles of similar things; and models, or the ways of thinking about causal relationships between categories.

- These perspectives, heuristics, categories, and models—but not identity differences—make diverse groups, teams, and cities more productive and more innovative. We do not solve problems with our identities; we solve them by thinking. However, our identities do influence how we think, so identity diversity can be lurking in the background throughout this course. In fact, identity diversity, training, experiences, and interests are all important drivers for cognitive diversity. They all contribute to how people see the world differently and how they think about specific problems differently.

- Diverse perspectives imply more possible solutions—as long as we have a way to evaluate them. That caveat aside, diverse teams are more innovative, more robust, and more able to respond to challenges and to trauma.

- In this course, you are going to observe myriad ways in which cognitive diversity operates in order to see how and why diversity contributes to collective performance. Cognitive differences are going to produce collective benefits through specific mechanisms—such as making mistakes less correlated—by giving us more solutions to possibly consider when we are trying to solve a problem using logic.

- When people talk about the benefits of diversity, they often mistakenly believe that there has to be some sort of synergy, which occurs when you add something together and you get something amazing as a result. For example, sodium and chlorine are both poisonous by themselves, but when we combine them in the right proportions, the result is table salt. Sometimes, with diverse groups of people, we get those synergies, but for diversity to be beneficial, we do not need synergies. In fact, the benefits of diversity are almost always inescapable; most of the time, diversity will be better than homogeneity without those synergies—but with the right types of diversity in the right amounts.

Recurring Course Ideas

- Efficiency, innovation, and **robustness** all require diversity. If we want a productive, interesting, sustainable world, we need to understand the role that diversity plays and maintain the right levels and types of diversity. Far too often, we think only in terms of talent, which matters, but collective performance depends on combining and growing diverse talent.

- Diversity—as it relates to people—is often framed in identity terms. Then, because much of politics involves dividing up resources, people mistakenly believe that they have to sacrifice something for the sake of diversity. More often, that is not true. In fact, most often, the opposite holds. We are not talking about who gets what share of a pie. Instead, we are talking about how to make a bigger and better pie—how to collectively tap into our diverse talents to find more innovative solutions and to respond better to challenges.

- The lessons in this course about diversity apply to you as an individual. You are an interesting, multifaceted person who possesses diverse skills and interests. In this course, you will hopefully discover how to tap into your own diversity and how diverse you should be. Hopefully, by the end of this course, you will learn how to be more productive, more innovative, and even more robust.

- This course relies on formal mathematical models, so some math is involved—but it won't be too complicated. Without math, we are stuck in a world of competing metaphors, such as "2 heads are better than 1" and "too many cooks spoil the broth." Formal models help us to understand the conditions necessary for 2 heads to be better than one. Models also help us to understand when those conditions do not hold so that we can boot some cooks out of the kitchen. Math helps us move past metaphors to eventually reach scientific understanding.

- Diversity makes life interesting. Diversity merits attention—even without pragmatic criteria like efficiency, accuracy, and robustness—because without it, life would be dull. Diversity is why London or New York is more exciting than an empty parking lot. It is why the Earth is more interesting than the Moon. It is why, after engaging in this course, you will be more interesting than you were before you took it.

- Interestingness depends on more than just lots of diversity. It is not just a matter of counting the number of types and concluding that more is better. Interestingness requires the proper connections and interactions among diverse parts. In the natural world, evolution has had a long time to subject variations and types to selective pressure in order to create the functioning assemblages known as ecosystems. In human systems, that assemblage problem—the creation of effective teams, groups, organizations, and societies—requires the work of intelligent, diverse thinkers.

Important Terms

category: A collection of similar events or objects.

cognitive diversity: Differences in the perspectives, heuristics, and categories that an individual uses to make predictions and find solutions to problems.

complex: A term used to describe a system that is between ordered and random and is difficult to explain, evolve, or predict.

diversity: Differences in types of entities.

heuristic: A technique or rule for finding improvements in the current best solution to a problem.

perspective: A representation of the set of possible solutions to a problem.

robustness: The ability of a complex system to maintain functionality given a disturbance or internal dynamics.

Suggested Reading

Page, *The Difference*, prologue and chap. 1.

————, *Diversity and Complexity*, prologue.

Questions to Consider

1. When someone mentions the word "diversity," do you think of it in political terms, or do you think of it more like a scientist?

2. Think of a scientific or logical basis for promoting greater diversity. What type of diversity does a scientific basis promote?

Why Now? The Rise of Diversity
Lecture 2

There are 2 fundamental trends that have made diversity increasingly important. First, within many countries—especially the United States—populations have become more diverse, inclusive, and open. Concurrently, connections across countries have strengthened and trade has increased as a result of modern technology. Second, as the economy in the United States and globally has transitioned from requiring many physical tasks to more cognitive ones, people are required to work together in teams that are diverse. Organizations are relying on teams because of the difficulty and complexity of the tasks that they face, and diverse people are working on difficult problems as a result.

Diversity Trends

- There are 2 main diversity trends that have led to increased interest in diversity. The first diversity trend is that American society is becoming more diverse. A majority of the children born in the United States are now nonwhite, which is a huge shift from 50 years ago. Relatedly, technology has reduced distance, and we are more connected. Our private and work lives intersect with a much more diverse set of people than they did in the past.

If each group member becomes specialized in a certain area of a task, the group is more effective at accomplishing the task.

- The second trend concerns the changing nature of work—specifically, the increased difficulty and the complexity of the challenges that we face in our work lives. This trend has produced a new reliance on teams, on group problem solving, and even on changes in the architecture of buildings.

- The simple explanation for the emergence of increasingly diverse teams is that we face difficult problems, so we need diverse teams, and we are now more diverse as a result. However, that explanation does not suffice because we are increasing in demographic diversity, which involve race and culture, but the challenges and opportunities before us require cognitive diversity, which are differences in how we think, so there is a disconnect—but only a partial one.

- Often, identity diversity and cognitive diversity are correlated. Therefore, the identity diversity of our work teams is going to imply a degree of cognitive diversity, which is going to make the teams better at what they do. On the other hand, identity diversity can also produce conflict, mistrust, and miscommunication—all of which can harm performance.

Identity Diversity

- Identity diversity is defined as differences in such characteristics as race, gender, cultural or ethnic background, and physical capabilities—differences in who we are. There are 2 broad reasons why identity diversity is becoming increasingly important: demographics and connectedness.

- From 1900 to 1940, approximately 90% of the population of the United States identified as being white. Almost all of the remainder of the population identified as being black, or African American. In 1970, the white proportion of the population still exceeded 80%, and the population classified as being of Hispanic origin was less than 5%. By 2010, the percentage of nonwhite Hispanics was less than 2/3 of the population, which is less than 66%. According to many estimates, by 2050, whites will no longer be a majority of the population.

- In terms of gender diversity, the percentage of men and women has not changed. However, as compared with women being absent from the work force 100 years ago, women now participate in nearly every sector of public and private life—in nearly as equal numbers as men. In fact, women now outnumber men at American colleges and universities. This inclusion in the work force extends beyond race and gender to other categories, such as physical challenges. People that were once considered incapable of holding meaningful jobs now participate in useful ways in the work force in record numbers.

- Furthermore, people are starting to accept diversity of other forms—such as religious belief and sexual orientation—which is allowing people in many cases to be open about their behaviors, opinions, and beliefs. This results in much greater expression of diversity than there was in the past.

- At the same time that we have a massive increase in diversity, we are also more connected. Advances in information technology and transportation reduce time and distance. Firms and markets are global, so goods that can be shipped compete with

The percentage of women versus men in society has not changed, but women are now more represented in the work force than they were 100 years ago.

each other in the marketplace on a day-to-day basis. In addition, on average, goods weigh less than they did previously. For example, information goods such as movies and songs have no weight and can be shipped at the speed of light. Greater diversity in products and in competitors result.

- From 1970 to 2000, the ratio of exports to world GDP rose from under 30% to over 40%. This means that a huge part of the world economy is now trade, which means more competition and more diversity.

- We can now connect with anyone, anywhere, anytime, and the people with whom we connect are probably going to be different from us. That is why there has been so much emphasis on diversity training and education in business.

Cognitive Diversity

- The reason that cognitive diversity—differences in how people think about problems—has become such a big deal relates to the changing nature of work. Specifically, it relates to how work increasingly involves less repetitive physical tasks and more thinking. In fact, 50 years ago, we thought of diversity in the workplace as **specialization**.

- The benefits of specialization involve the idea of learning by doing—the notion that as people specialize, they learn faster and are more productive—and the trade that follows specialization. If people specialize, then they get better faster and they can do the thing that they are best at and reap the enormous benefits they get through trade. These insights provide the traditional foundation for why diversity produces value.

- When individuals, regions, or countries specialize in some particular good, product, or service, they can trade those things for other things that they need. In this way, each country can focus on the things that they are really good at and trade for the things that they need. Economists refer to this as the **theory of comparative advantage**, in which relative abilities—not absolute abilities—are what matter.

- Over the past 100 years, work has become less physical and more cognitive. From 1910 to 1970, the U.S. economy consisted mostly of manufacturing. In 1950, over 1/3 of U.S. jobs were in manufacturing. By 2010, that number was less than 1/6.

- Total employment in manufacturing in the United States peaked in the late 1970s, but there is the same number of manufacturing workers today as there were in 1940, when the population was 1/2 of what it is today. Those manufacturing workers have moved into other jobs.

- People can make stuff, they can service, or they can think. Economists refer to the first 2 as the manufacturing and service sectors, respectively. The third sector is still searching for a name but has several. Economist Richard Florida calls these workers "the creative class" while economist Robert Reich calls them "cognitive workers."

- Manufacturing is falling and the creative class is rising, and this trend correlates with the increase in cognitive diversity because of the following logic.
  o Creative people solve, design, and predict.
  o The problems that creative people confront are challenging.
  o Many of these problems outstrip the capabilities of any one person, which means that creative people have to form groups. When they form groups, they form groups of people that are cognitively diverse. If group members were not different from you—if they did not think differently—then they would not help you. You would not need more than one person in the group.

- The point is that 2 heads are only going to be better than one if the heads differ. We need cognitive diversity when problems are difficult. In other words, we do not need cognitive diversity when problems are easy. It is when the problem becomes difficult that we turn to groups, teams, or even crowds.

Difficult versus Complex Problems

- The term "difficult" refers to high-dimensional problems—those with lots of variables and interactions between the various choices and variables that we have to make. We have always faced difficult problems, but the number of difficult problems is on the rise because we have solved most of the easy problems and are left with the more difficult ones.

- The other reason that problems have become harder is that new technologies allow us to see the world at finer levels of granularity, exposing more dimensions. Problems that once were unassailable are now a large part of our economy—such as creating molecules to cure diseases, designing microprocessors, and writing software— and comprise an ever-growing chunk of the creative class's work time.

- In addition to difficulty, rising complexity has led to an increased interest in diversity. A system is said to be "complex" if it is somewhere between ordered and completely random. Complex systems—such as ecosystems, economies, and political systems— are difficult to design, explain, engineer, and predict. The types of systems that produce complexity consist of a few common attributes: They have diverse parts that are interconnected, they are **interdependent** in their actions, and they adapt to one another.

- Many of the challenges that we face—constructing robust financial systems, reducing poverty, improving education, managing the climate, and improving transportation—can all be thought of as complex. Each day, we have to confront these problems anew. That is not true of difficult problems. Once you have solved a difficult problem, you can move on to something else.

- Businesses have always had to adapt, but thanks to information and communication technology, the rate at which they have to adapt has changed dramatically. Companies used to wait 30 to 90 days to see what products were selling in markets, but they now know instantaneously because they can obtain that data immediately at corporate headquarters.

- In complex, constantly changing environments, diversity becomes crucial. How diversity works, though, is fundamentally different from how it did in the past. In the past, what we were doing was based on scientific management techniques. A problem was broken into parts, and then people specialized in those parts. In the traditional model, specialization meant isolation. People had diverse skills, but those diverse skills were not interacting directly—they were separated by space and time.

- Modern specialization—cognitive specialization—relies on direct interaction. On difficult and complex tasks, we tend to work together, and we tend to be in the same room. When we work together, we confront cognitive diversity.

Important Terms

interdependence: The influence of one entity's action on the behavior, payoff, or fitness of another entity.

specialization: The practice of having individuals perform a single task so that they can improve at that task.

theory of comparative advantage: A theory that shows how 2 countries can both benefit from trade, provided each is relatively better at producing some good.

Suggested Reading

Florida, *The Rise of the Creative Class*.

Page, *Diversity and Complexity*, chap. 8.

Questions to Consider

1. How do specialization and trade create incentives for diversity?

2. What is different about the gains from specialization in a production economy and a cognitive economy?

Diversity Squared
Lecture 3

In this lecture, you will learn that the path to diversity is a 5-step process, starting with the framing of identity differences as morally and legally valued. You will also learn that equal opportunity and affirmative action created a bigger pool and that once the pool was integrated, many groups and organizations discovered a diversity bonus. Then, you will learn that people began to restructure as a result of the diversity bonus. Much of this course will consist of trying to figure out when that bonus exists and how to leverage it so that we can make the world better.

Moral and Legal Equality

- People think about diversity very differently, and how we think about diversity is undergoing a huge society-wide transformation. This transformation does not have anything to do with political ideology; instead, it is based on pragmatism and personal experience.

- In the United States, the rise in diversity thinking is a result of the confluence of 2 trends: increased identity diversity and increased team-based work. That means that people now have more interactions with identity-diverse people. It is those interactions that have led to a rethinking, and that rethinking has happened in 5 stages: moral equality, legal equality, the bigger pool, the diversity bonus, and restructuring.

- The path to diversity starts with recognizing the moral component of equality thinking. Moral arguments for equality are referenced in many old religious texts, where there is often a focus on seeing people for who they are internally—not for external differences. In other words, we differ in how we look, but we should recognize the abilities in each of us and treat one another fairly and with respect.

- In the United States, we have a long, troubled history in our attempts to treat one another equally. Consider our experience with slavery, the Civil War, the women's suffrage movement, and the civil rights movement. We could have treated one another with more respect.

- One can read U.S. history as a struggle for inclusiveness. Many see the 1960s, for a variety of reasons, as a watershed period—as a time when we began to embrace the moral argument fully. We responded to citizens' cries for equality with laws of legal equality. This comprised the second stage on the path to diversity. President Johnson pushed through civil rights legislation that made discrimination based on race and gender illegal. However, inequality did not stop immediately; it takes time for words on paper to change behavior.

The American civil rights protests of the 1950s and 1960s led to the end of racial segregation and, eventually, to the integration of all races in society.

The Bigger Pool

- The change in the law resulted in changes that were worthwhile: a more diverse workforce and a more diverse society. That experience led to the third stage toward diversity, called the bigger pool logic, which is the notion that people of every identity group bring talent. In this stage, schools, organizations, businesses, and voters began to recognize that talent could be found in people of any race, gender, ethnicity, sexual orientation, and religion. As we opened up our doors to everyone, we realized that we could access more talent.

- The bigger pool logic shifts the argument from moral grounds to pragmatic grounds. One could then make an argument for diversity solely on pragmatic grounds: Equality of opportunity would produce better outcomes by opening up a larger talent pool. Firms and organizations that hired women and people of color would have access to more talent, so in the long run, they are going to outperform their competitors because the talent is going to win out.

- This realization did not make all the issues related to diversity and inclusion disappear, however. There were 3 problems that remained, and they still remain today. We will refer to them as the starting line, the smart-just-like-me effect, and structural discrimination.

- The starting line argument states that you cannot give one group—in this case white men—a 50-yard head start in a 100-yard dash and then have a race. Equality now is not sufficient to redress past discrimination.

- The smart-just-like-me effect involves the fact that people tend to be more comfortable around people who look like them and think like they do. Therefore, we tend to undervalue diversity. Most people have a slight preference for working with people who look like themselves, and this often puts women and minorities—and other historically disadvantaged groups—at a disadvantage because in the evaluation of 2 equal candidates, we bias in favor of the one who looks like the person in charge.

- Structural discrimination refers to policies and procedures put in place for entirely different reasons that end up producing discriminatory outcomes even though no one wanted them. For example, many colleges and universities set aside seats for legacies, or students whose parents attended the school or whose parents work at the school. The problem is that if the institution used to be biased against some ethnic group, these legacy programs are going to maintain that bias—and they will continue to do so for centuries.

- The starting line effect, the smart-just-like-me effect, and the structural discrimination effect led to the creation of affirmative action programs because the idea was that we needed to somehow make these programs more equal. Affirmative action gave members of underrepresented groups advantages to equalize opportunity. Affirmative action had, and continues to have, many critics. Those against it argue that you do not fix a wrong with another wrong; in this case, the second wrong is discrimination against the majority group.

- Even though there are many issues with it, the bigger pool logic separates talent from identity, putting the focus on talent. By this logic, an organization should be diverse because if it wants talent, it should be blind to color and gender. In addition, with the bigger pool logic, performance depends entirely on talent, which is independent of diversity.

- The interesting part is that identity diversity often correlated with cognitive diversity. People who live different lives and have different experiences tend to think differently, so the best teams in the workplace often turned out to be diverse teams. As a result, this led people to seek out diversity for performance reasons.

The Diversity Bonus
- The diversity bonus has 2 parts: Identity diversity often correlates with or produces cognitive diversity, and cognitive diversity improves collective performance. We are going to focus on the second part, and we are going to discover that it is too broad and imprecise. It does not explain what cognitive diversity is, and it does not say what types of collective performance it is going to improve, how much it will improve them, and through what mechanisms.

- Evidence suggests that our identities influence how we think in 2 fundamental ways: We filter many of our experiences and our interpretations through our identities, and the experiences and opportunities that we have differ based on our identity.

In 1964, President Lyndon B. Johnson signed the Civil Rights Act, which resulted in the end of legal discrimination on the basis of race, color, religion, or national origin.

- Try as we might, people are not blind to identity. We are aware of someone's gender, ethnicity, and age, and as a result, we tend to treat people differently. For example, most of us tend to be more comfortable with people from our own identity group, so we're more open around people who are similar to us. This means that we all experience slightly different realities as a function of who we are.

- If people from distinct identity groups have different experiences, then they will think differently about the world. In addition, if people think differently about the world, then even if they have identical experiences, they may filter them differently, so it'll be as if they are different experiences. Thus, identity diversity and cognitive differences must be related. How much they are related and the linkages between the various types of identity diversity and cognitive diversity will depend on the types of identity diversity we're considering and on the cognitive task.

- Our cultural identities influence the stories we hear, the books we read, the movies we watch, and the music we listen to. Cultures also influence the set of parables and myths that we hear. These, in turn, become the analogies we use to make sense of the world. Thus, our ethnicity plays a substantial role in our basic cognitive building blocks.

- Identity contributes to our experiences, to how we see the world, and to how we're taught—and all of these contribute to cognitive diversity. In some cases, that cognitive diversity is germane, but in other cases, it may not be.

- One should expect that often both parts of the argument should hold: A group, team, or organization that is identity diverse will have relevant cognitive diversity, and that group, team, or organization, will be better at a cognitive task. That's the diversity bonus. Note that the diversity bonus comes from the second part of the logic—cognitive diversity's ability to improve collective performance. Identity diversity often correlates with cognitive diversity, but it has no direct effect.

- One could fill hundreds of hours with anecdotes, case studies, and summaries of empirical research demonstrating the diversity bonus and linking the bonus to identity. On the other hand, one could also fill the same amount of time with research showing the opposite—that identity diverse groups fail miserably. There are, in fact, productive diverse groups and unproductive diverse groups.

- Robin Ely and David Thomas, who have studied diverse team performance, have found that attitudes matter and that, to a degree, they prove self-fulfilling. If you expect diversity to lead to better solutions, you will find that it does. If you don't, then you'll likely be part of a dysfunctional group.

Restructuring

- Attaining functional diversity often requires restructuring—changing the way things are done. Consider that an organization has a problem, such as reducing electricity costs or saving space, for which it's possible to determine immediately (and at no cost) whether an idea works. Talent logic would suggest that it makes no sense for the firm to open up this question to less talented people because they would have little to add. However, diversity logic would suggest that anyone might have a good idea because each person might bring different ways of thinking and could make an improvement. Therefore, the organization should—provided that it's not too costly—let anyone propose solutions, which would require restructuring and the sharing of power. Unfortunately, this type of disruption is not always acceptable to everyone.

- It's possible to restructure so that groups and teams exhibit identity diversity as well as cognitive diversity. If you have an identity-diverse team, you have no guarantee of cognitive diversity or that you have the appropriate types for the task at hand, but your prior belief should be that there's probably some cognitive diversity. Alternatively, if the room is filled with people who all look the same, you question whether there exists sufficient cognitive diversity.

Questions to Consider

1. What are the 5 stages in the diversity journey?

2. Why does thinking about the diversity bonus often entail restructuring or disruption in standard practices?

The Wisdom of Crowds
Lecture 4

In this lecture, you will observe how diverse ways of thinking contribute to the ability of a collection of people to make accurate predictions. This phenomenon, called the wisdom of crowds, occurs when a crowd of people is more accurate than the people in it. Upon examining the wisdom of crowds, you will learn that it depends on 2 things: talent (good predictors) and diversity. In fact, the collective accuracy of a crowd depends in equal measure on the accuracy of its members and on their diversity. Furthermore, a diverse crowd will always be more accurate than its average member.

Diverse Predictions

- One of the most famous examples of the wisdom of crowds involves guessing the weight of cattle. The example is due to Sir Francis Galton, who collected data on 787 people who guessed the weight of a steer. Their average guess of the weight of the steer was 1197 pounds. Amazingly, the actual weight of the steer was 1198 pounds. Galton's cattle contest is a single example; it by no means implies that in every instance a crowd will predict with such incredible accuracy. In fact, crowds often make mistakes, just like individuals do. However, the evidence—from not just cattle guessing, but also from the trenches of the business and policy worlds—is that although Galton's example is amazing, it has a grain of truth.

- Suppose that Amy, Belle, and Carlos make predictions regarding the number of new clients that a firm will attract in the next year. If Amy guesses 12, Belle guesses 6, and Carlos guesses 15, then the average guess is 12 plus 6 plus 15, which equals 33, divided by 3 for an average of 11. Suppose that the actual number of new clients will turn out to be 10.

- We need some way of measuring the accuracy of the individuals as well as the accuracy of the crowd. Statisticians typically do this by taking the difference between the actual prediction and the true value and squaring that amount. They call the result the squared error. Squaring the errors makes all errors positive and prevents them from cancelling one another.

- ○ Amy's squared error equals $(12-10)^2$, or 4.
- ○ Belle's squared error equals $(6-10)^2$, or 16.
- ○ And Carlos' squared error equals $(15-10)^2$, or 25.

- The average of these squared errors equals 4 plus 16 plus 25 divided by 3, which is 45 divided by 3, or 15. Therefore, the average individual squared error equals 15.

- The crowd's error equals $(11-10)^2$, or 1. Therefore, the crowd's squared error equals 1.

- In this example, the crowd is more accurate than individuals are on average, and the crowd is also more accurate than any member of the crowd. The latter won't always be true. Someone in the crowd can be more accurate than the crowd. However, the crowd is always more accurate than its average member.

- Next, we need some way of measuring the diversity of the crowd's predictions. Statistics has a standard approach: We just square the difference between the predictions and the mean prediction.

- Recall that the mean, or average, prediction was eleven.
  - ○ Amy's squared difference from the mean equals $(12-11)^2$, or 1.
  - ○ Belle's squared difference from the mean equals $(6-11)^2$, or 25.
  - ○ Carlos's squared difference from the mean equals $(15-11)^2$, or 16.

- If you add these 3 numbers, you obtain 42. If you then divide by 2, you get an average squared difference from the mean (also called diversity of the predictions) of 14.

- The crowd's squared error equals the average individual squared error minus the diversity of the predictions. This is called the **diversity prediction theorem**, and it is true not just for this example, but for every example. This is an important and counterintuitive result: The crowd's ability depends in equal measure on ability and diversity.

The Diversity Prediction Theorem
- Suppose that there exists some future or unknown value (x) that a crowd of people must predict, such as an unemployment rate or the number of jelly beans in a jar. Suppose that n people are making predictions. We can label these people from 1 to n and index them so that x_i equals the prediction of person i.

- The crowd's prediction, C, equals the average of the individual predictions. Mathematically, we can write that as

$$C = \frac{1}{n}\left(x_1 + x_2 + \ldots x_n\right).$$

- Then, we can use a summation sign (the Greek letter sigma), which tells us to sum all of the x_i terms:

$$C = \frac{1}{n}\sum_{i=1}^{n} x_i.$$

- The crowd's squared error (CE^2) equals the square of the difference between C (the collective prediction) and x (the truth): $CE^2 = (C - x)^2$.

- The average squared error equals the sum of the individual squared errors. Person i's squared error equals the difference between that person's prediction, x_i, and the true value x. Therefore, the average individual squared error (IE^2) equals the sum of all of those terms divided by n:

$$IE^2 = \frac{1}{n}\sum_{i=1}^{n}\left(x_i - x\right)^2.$$

- Finally, the diversity of the predictions (D_p) equals the average squared difference between the predictions and the collective prediction C:

$$D_P = \frac{1}{n}\sum_{i=1}^{n}(x_i - C)^2.$$

- We can now state the formal theorem: $CE^2 = IE^2 - D_p$.

- Using the explicit mathematical expressions,

$$(C - x)^2 = \left[\frac{1}{n}\sum_{i=1}^{n}(x_i - x)^2\right] - \left[\frac{1}{n}\sum_{i=1}^{n}(x_i - C)^2\right].$$

- Both of these expressions mean that crowd error equals average individual error minus diversity. For any collection of predictions, this will hold. It's a mathematical identity.

- In other words, the wisdom of crowds—the ability of crowds to make accurate collective predictions—depends in equal measure on the crowd's ability (their averaged individual squared error) and the diversity of their predictions.

- If the crowd's squared error equals the average individual squared error minus the diversity of the predictions, then the corollary is also true: If the crowd has any diversity in its predictions, then the crowd's error is strictly less than the average squared error of the people in the crowd. This is referred to as the crowd-beats-the-average law.

- The crowd's error equals the average individual error—the diversity. Therefore, if diversity is positive, the crowd's error will always be smaller. On average, crowds are better than the people that comprise them.

- If you a want a wise crowd, you have 2 options: Find all brilliant people who know the answer (error = 0, and diversity = 0), or find a bunch of smart people (error = moderate) who differ (diversity = moderate). If you take any example from books on wise crowds where the crowd is freakishly accurate, the latter always holds. In other words, in cases that deal with the wisdom of crowds, crowd error equals average error minus diversity.

- Small crowd error equals moderately large average individual error minus lots of diversity. If it were true that small crowd error equals small individual error minus almost no diversity of predictions, then the crowd would be correct because everyone in the crowd was correct. There wouldn't be any wisdom of the crowd. Instead, it would just be a group of people who know the answer.

Understanding the Diversity Prediction Theorem

- Suppose that there is a crowd of 100 people guessing the weight of a steer, and suppose that each person is off by exactly 20 pounds. If the steer weighs 1060, that means that each person guesses either 1040 or 1080.

- Suppose there's no predictive diversity—that everyone guesses 1040. The crowd's guess will be 1040, so the crowd's squared error will be 400. Each individual will also have a squared error equal to 400, so the average individual squared error will also equal 400, and the diversity equals 0.

- Plugging this into the formula, you get 400 = 400 − 0.

- Next, suppose that the predictions are more diverse—that 1/2 of the people guess 1040 and 1/2 guess 1080. This time, the crowd gets it exactly right. Notice that the average individual squared error has not changed; it's still 400. However, when you plug these values into the diversity prediction theorem, you get 0 = 400 − 400.

- The people didn't become smarter, but the crowd did—because it became more diverse.

- Suppose that there is a crowd that is not wise. Then, a large crowd error results, which means that there is also a large average individual error. It also means that diversity has to be relatively small; otherwise, the diversity would cancel out the errors. If diversity weren't small relative to the error, the crowd wouldn't be unwise.

Where Does Diversity Come From?
- People make different predictions because they have different conceptual models of how the world works. This tendency for people to base predictions on what they know is called base-rate bias. We're influenced by how we start thinking about a problem. Therefore, the crowd gets it right because the idiosyncratic errors of the individuals cancel. Idiosyncratic errors should be equally likely to be high or low; therefore, they'll be diverse—leading to a wise crowd.

- Suppose that you go to a meeting in which you're tasked to predict something, such as the number of attendees at an event, the sales of a new product, the price of a stock, or the rate of unemployment. Consider 2 scenarios.
  - Scenario 1: You go to the meeting and everyone agrees. You all make nearly identical predictions and use similar logic.
  - Scenario 2: The predictions differ because people use different models.

- In scenario 1, there are 2 possibilities: Either everyone is wrong, or everyone is right. If it's a hard problem, it may not be likely that everyone is right. The only way that you should feel good about the outcome is if you feel that this was an easy predictive task, and if it was an easy predictive task, then there was no reason for the crowd. Everyone will get it right, so there's no need for diversity.

- In scenario 2, there's disagreement. Some people think that sales will be high while others think that sales will be low. By the corollary to the diversity prediction theorem, the crowd will be more accurate than its average member. Therefore, after you leave the meeting, you should feel good because the crowd definitely made a better prediction than some random person from the group would have made on his or her own.

- In other words, if you go to a meeting in which you are predicting something, the fact that people disagree is good. It means that there is diversity in the room, and diversity improves performance. It's a mathematical truism.

Important Term

diversity prediction theorem: The collective error for a crowd equals the average error minus the diversity of the predictions.

Suggested Reading

Page, *The Difference*, chap. 8.

Suroweicki, *The Wisdom of Crowds*.

Questions to Consider

1. Describe the diversity prediction theorem.

2. Use the diversity prediction theorem to explain why the crowd is always smarter than the average person in it.

The Diversity Prediction Theorem Times Three
Lecture 5

In this lecture, you're going to learn about an application of forecasting—namely, using knowledge of a population to better serve that population—by studying a particular case that involves Netflix. On predictive tasks, individual talent and collective diversity matter equally. Finding more talented people may often be more difficult than finding people of approximately equal talent who think differently. Other people's opinions may be no more accurate than our own, but if they're different and we combine them with our own, we will predict more accurately, allowing us to see a little bit farther down the road.

Forecasting: A Case Study

- On October 2, 2006, Reed Hastings, the CEO of Netflix—an online movie rental company—began the million-dollar Netflix Prize competition. Netflix had developed a computer algorithm called Cinematch, which predicted movie preferences. The contest rules were simple: Be 10% better at forecasting someone's ratings than Cinematch and win a million dollars.

- Suppose, for example, that you had rented *The Sting*, a 1970s classic starring Robert Redford and Paul Newman, and that on the Netflix website, you gave that movie a rating of 5 stars, meaning that you loved it. Then, based on the nature of that movie—and perhaps on some demographic information—Cinematch would make some predictions. For example, it might predict that you would also give 5 stars to the movie *Butch Cassidy and the Sundance Kid*, another Redford-Newman buddy film loaded with intrigue and witty banter.

- Alternatively, suppose that you had rented *8 Mile*, a gritty film about Detroit rappers. If you liked that film, Cinematch might predict that you wouldn't like *Butch Cassidy and the Sundance Kid*, but that you would like the movie *Men in Black*, starring Tommy Lee Jones and Will Smith, who is a rapper.

- If you run Netflix, an accurate Cinematch gives you what economists call market power. If you can predict the movie preferences of one of your members, then that member will be less likely to abandon Netflix for some other movie rental site. This is because when a member is deciding on a movie, Netflix will show the member a predicted customized rating of 1 to 5 stars for that movie based on his or her previous ratings of other movies. Over time, Cinematch will learn what types of movies the member likes and dislikes.

- The Netflix Prize was a forecasting competition with large stakes. As a result, it attracted some of the best and the brightest, including scientists from the former Bell Laboratories, professors, postdocs, and graduate students from some of the top universities in the world. In effect, this was a competition to see who could construct the best model, and that turned out to be a diverse team.

Background

- Netflix offered over 100 million rankings by about 1/2 of a million users who had rated nearly 18,000 movies. All together, the data consisted of more than 100 million individual movie ratings. The contest organizers divided that data randomly into 2 sets: a training set and a testing set. The testing set included only about 3 million ratings. Netflix then put the training set out on the web. This contained information about each movie, each renter, and each rating. Individuals and teams used this training set to construct their predictive models.

- Once someone had developed a model, they could apply it to the testing set, which was another set of data that did not include the ratings. This allowed competitors to test how well their models worked. This testing set was broken into 3 sets: one to do practice tests on, one used for formal rankings, and a third that was kept for the final validation that would be used to determine the winner. These testing sets were small relative to the training sets—each of the 3 had about 1.5 million movie ratings.

- Beating Cinematch was easy. Within a week, a group called WXYZ had done so. However, beating Cinematch by 10% proved to be difficult.

Nearest-Neighbor and Decomposition Methods

- Early in the competition, competitors used a variety of modeling approaches. At first, the model method that was relied on was nearest-neighbor methods. For each pair of movies, participants created a similarity measure. For example, *Rocky II* would be very similar to *Rocky* but not very similar to *Gone with the Wind*. The estimate for how a person rated a movie was determined by how that person had rated similar movies.

- Soon, however, the best model methods relied on decomposition methods. For example, James Cameron's *Titanic* can be broken into a long list of attributes, including romance, drama, disaster/death, huge budget, blockbuster in sales, syrupy music videos, and historical. This list is called the vector of attributes.

- To determine whether a person will like a particular movie, we need to know whether the person likes particular attributes. We can do this by estimating a vector of preferences over attributes for each person. For example, we can make these preferences numbers between 0 and 10. A number 0 for an attribute means that the person does not at all like that attribute, and a number 10 means that he or she loves it.

- A hypothetical movie renter might have the following preferences over the attributes that we just listed.
  - romance = 7
  - drama = 9
  - disaster/death = 2
  - huge budget = 2
  - blockbuster in sales = 8
  - syrupy music videos = 4
  - historical = 10

- We can then add up all these numbers and make a prediction of how much the hypothetical movie renter will like *Titanic*. In addition, we might want to add 2 other features called dummy variables by statisticians. The first dummy variable will be a movie dummy, which takes into account the average rating of the movie by other people. This variable will give a bonus for good movies and subtract from bad movies. The other dummy will be a person dummy, which corrects for whether an individual tends to give high ratings or low ratings. Some people might give only 4 or 5 stars while others may give mostly 1s and 2s. The person dummy corrects for this.

- A good model will identify the attributes that matter—attributes that have high information content. A bad model will be one that does not.

- Matrix decomposition methods work similar to this, except that an algorithm takes in all the data about the movies and determines the attributes. In effect, you plug in all sorts of features for a movie, and a computer algorithm constructs latent factors. These factors condense a whole bunch of features into a single dimension. For example, a movie that includes a car chase may also tend to include suspense and bombs. These 3 features might all get lumped into a single latent factor.

- These matrix methods require you to determine how many latent factors, or attributes, to consider. The early leader in the competition, BellKor (formerly known as Bell Laboratories), used from 50 up to 200 factors. They also allowed people's preferences, the weights that they attached to each attribute, to change over time. This enabled them to account for someone's tastes changing.

BellKor's Model

- The BellKor team was led by Robert Bell. BellKor's best model used approximately 50 variables per movie. BellKor's best model could improve on Cinematch by about 6.58%. However, BellKor had more than one model. In fact, they had 107. When they blended those models together, they could get up to an 8.43% improvement.

- Remember that the diversity prediction theorem states that the crowd's error equals average error minus diversity. BellKor had a crowd of models, and by combining them, BellKor could do even better.

- The diversity prediction theorem considers errors, and smaller errors correspond to better models. With the Netflix Prize competition, we're talking about percent improvement. Thus, larger percentage improvements imply better models. A good crowd of models will depend on those models being individually accurate and collectively diverse.

- With the diversity prediction theorem, we assume that all of the models get weighted equally, but in practice, one can do much better. Intuitively, by putting more weight on better models and less weight on weaker models, the crowd can do even better. However, in the extreme, this would imply that the best model will be better than some weighted average of the crowd, and that's typically not true.

- In this case, it was decidedly not true; a weighted average of BellKor's models improved on Cinematch by 8.43%. Netflix gave out a small prize, $50,000, to the team leading at the end of each year. BellKor won in 2007.

The Path to the Prize

- In 2008, BellKor decided to become more diverse. They joined forces with a team called BigChaos, 2 computer scientists from Austria. This team had developed ways to combine models nonlinearly. Rather than just putting weights on models and adding their predictions, BigChaos used more sophisticated techniques for aggregating.

- In 2009, the team added Pragmatic Theory, a group of Canadians who were experts in modeling how preferences change. This new team was called BellKor's Pragmatic Chaos. When they combined their models, they had more than 800 variables.

- With more attributes to include in their models, the members of BellKor's Pragmatic Chaos were able to build more accurate individual models. In fact, they were able to build one model that proved to be as accurate as their previous blend of models—an 8.4% improvement.

- Furthermore, when they blended these improved and diverse models to form what computer scientists call an ensemble of models, they broke 10%. On June 26, 2009, more than 2 years after the contest began, they won a million dollars, which would go to public schools in New Jersey.

- Contest rules stated that once someone broke the 10% barrier, the contest would end in 30 days. Reed Hastings included this extra period to ensure that the contest would be interesting and that he would get a really great solution. Therefore, BellKor's Pragmatic Chaos had to wait.

- The other teams were talented as well. In hopes that their diversity would help them beat BellKor, the other teams formed a team called The Ensemble. Given the limited amount of time left in the contest, The Ensemble strategically looked for the best possible blend of models. With just 2 days to go, they beat BellKor's Pragmatic Chaos. The Ensemble's extraordinary diversity served them well.

- With both teams above 10% and the clock ticking down, each submitted its final model. BellKor won on the fifth decimal point. However, the fifth decimal point hardly counts as significant in a statistical sense. For this reason, the rules said that only the first 4 decimal points counted. Thus, there was a tie. The tiebreaker called for the winner to be the team that submitted their model first, and BellKor's Pragmatic Chaos won by 22 minutes.

- Because the 2 final models that were submitted differ, combining them leads to an even greater improvement than either one was able to display individually.

Suggested Reading

Bell, Koren, and Volinsky, "All Together Now."

Questions to Consider

1. Describe 3 times when the diversity prediction theorem was in action during the Netflix Prize competition.

2. What does the success of The Ensemble say about the relative value of diversity and ability?

The Weighting Is the Hardest Part
Lecture 6

Determining how much you listen to some predictors at the expense of others requires careful thinking. Accuracy matters, but you must be accurate about who you think is accurate. Diversity also matters, but you must make sure that you recognize germane diversity of thought. Attaching correct differential weight to various predictors takes experience, practice, knowledge of the problem, and the accuracy and diversity of the predictors. Knowing the advantages—and being aware of the pitfalls—of weighting will make you better able to make judicious assignments.

The Optimal Weighting Theory

- Multiple models are better than one, but it also stands to reason that when you listen to multiple models and some seem more reasonable than others, you should heed the better models. However, if you take this logic to its logical conclusion, then you should place all of the weight on the most accurate person. Unfortunately, this seems to run counter to the diversity prediction theorem.

- According to the diversity prediction theorem, as we place more weight on the better predictors, we decrease average error. However, in doing so, we reduce diversity. If the gain in error reduction exceeds the loss of diversity, then our prediction will be more accurate. If not, then we should not place more weight on better predictors—even though they are better.

- The question of weighting predictions can be considered as 2 separate questions: Whom should we include? Once we've decided who belongs to the group, how much weight do we attach to each one?

- Imagine that the 3 predictors from a previous lecture—Amy, Belle, and Carlos—have been making predictions for several years and that we have accumulated data on their squared errors. Suppose that Amy's looks as follows: 49, 64, 16, 1, 49, 1. If we add this up, we get an average of 30. This is her average individual squared error. Statisticians call this **variance**.

- Suppose that we have the following variance estimates for each of these 3 people: Amy = 30, Belle = 15, and Carlos = 60. In statistics, the accuracy of a prediction equals the inverse of the variance. If there is high variance, then there is low accuracy; if there is low variance, then there is high accuracy. If the variance were 0, it would have infinite accuracy.

- Amy's accuracy equals 1/30, Belle's equals 1/25, and Carlos's equals 1/60. All we need to keep track of is relative accuracy, so we can multiply each of these accuracies by 60, which results in the following: Amy's accuracy = 2, Belle's accuracy = 4, and Carlos's accuracy = 1.

- By using calculus, one can show that the optimal set of weights— the weights that produce the minimal squared error—should be proportional to the accuracy of the predictions.

- Amy's weight equals her accuracy (2) divided by the sum of the accuracies, which is $2 + 4 + 1$, or 7. Therefore, Amy's weight equals 2/7. Similarly, Belle's weight equals 4/7, and Carlos's weight equals only 1/7 because he is the least accurate. As a result, more accurate predictors get more weight.

- These calculations assume that the predictions satisfy a condition called independence, which implies that knowing one person's prediction tells you nothing about another person's prediction. Independence assumes substantial diversity between the predictions; it's saying that one prediction contains no information about the other.

- Because we have 3 people, the independence assumption implies that Belle's prediction is no more like Carlos's prediction than it is like Amy's. In general, this might not be true. One pair of 2 predictions might be more similar than another pair.

- If Amy and Belle's predictions tend to be alike but Carlos's tends to be substantially different, then Carlos's prediction will have less correlation with Amy's prediction than Amy's prediction has with Belle's.

In a group setting, the more diverse the potential contributors are, the more useful they can be to the group as a whole.

Correlation captures similarity. If the correlation is positive, then predictions are similar. If it is negative, then the predictions tend to be different. If it is 0, then they are independent. Independence, or zero correlation, is a convenient assumption, but it usually won't hold.

- If we take correlation into account, we can assign even better weights. The less correlated a predictor is with the others, the more diverse his or her predictions will be and the more weight that he or she should receive. The more correlated a predictor is with the others, the less weight he or she should get.

- With the diversity prediction theorem, collective accuracy depends on individual accuracy and diversity. Optimal weighting theory reinforces this same logic: More accurate predictors should receive more weight—as should more diverse predictors.

- By assigning weights correctly, we can both increase accuracy and increase diversity. If we can do that, then we can increase collective accuracy in 2 ways. In effect, by shifting weights, it's as if we make the individuals both more accurate and more diverse.

From Theory to Practice

- The optimal weighting theory is a mathematical identity, but unlike the diversity prediction theorem, it relies on being able to know the correlation of the predictions—which we may not know. If we know the correlations with a high degree of accuracy, then we should be able to do better by assigning weights. If we don't know those statistics with much accuracy, then weighting can be problematic.

- To avoid complicating matters, consider only accuracy, leaving diversity and correlation out of the picture. Suppose that there are only 2 predictors: Amy and Belle. Recall that Belle's accuracy was twice Amy's. Using the weighting formula, Amy's weight should equal $1/(1 + 2)$, or $1/3$, and Belle's should equal $2/3$, so we place more weight on Belle.

- However, suppose that Belle proves to be no more accurate than Amy—that Belle just randomly happened to predict more accurately on her first 6 predictions. That would mean that by placing more weight on Belle, we would lose diversity but not gain any accuracy. If that's the case, then by weighting, we would do worse. By attaching more weight to people who just happen to have done better, we make the collective prediction less accurate. For this reason, unequal weighting suddenly looks less attractive.

- Models that are like other models, even if they are accurate, get less weight. Optimal weights depend much more on a model's diversity than on its accuracy. Diversity matters so much that some highly accurate models get negative weight because they have to cancel out the duplication of the other models.

- In practice, you have to distinguish between 2 types of situations. In the first, you don't have that much data on past experience, and some predictors seem a little more accurate than others. In these cases, unless you have strong evidence, equal weighting is not a bad choice—although you may want to abandon models that haven't been at all useful.

- In the second type of situation, when you have lots and lots of data on past performance, then you can take into account ability and place more weight on the more accurate models, but the mathematics suggests that you would do better by also considering the diversity of the models. This can be done by taking the past data and breaking it into 2 sets: a training set and a testing set. On the training set, you explore different combinations of predictors to see which weights give you the most accurate predictions. After you've come up with what you think are a good set of weights, you can then verify that it proves more accurate on the testing set as well.

- When you don't have any past data, in order to weight the opinions of the people involved, you have to consider the proxies for accuracy that you might have. Proxies for accuracy might be past record or the strength of the argument. Both of these might lead you to put more weight on someone's opinion.

- In other words, reputation, status, and charisma should not matter. If someone's status or reputation resulted from consistently making good forecasts, then you could give his or her opinion more weight, but you need a reason.

- In terms of diversity, if you think about how different the models are and place more weight on models that offer compelling but distinct logic, you should be careful not to place too much weight on any one model. Otherwise, you lose much of the wisdom of crowds. Focus on the diversity of the models—not the diversity of the numerical predictions.

Whom Should We Include?

- At the most basic level, the diversity prediction theorem informs us that we should add someone to the prediction pool if his or her net effect on accuracy minus diversity is positive. A no-brainer addition would be someone who would both increase average accuracy and increase diversity. However, such people will be rare. More often, someone will either increase accuracy but decrease diversity or will decrease accuracy and increase diversity.

- The first type—the higher accuracy predictors—tend to be more acceptable to groups and teams. Few people complain about adding someone to a group who is better than the average group member at the task. However, the second type—someone who is less accurate than the average team member but diverse—can add just as much value, but they can be a harder sell to the team.

- Suppose that you run a chain of retail establishments, such as electronic stores, restaurants, or bookstores. On a regular basis, you need to forecast sales of new products. For years, you've relied on an in-house market researcher, but you've read some books about the wisdom of crowds and decide to use a crowd of market researchers and store managers to make sales forecasts.

- You have 2 populations: market researchers and store managers. Market researchers will be highly accurate, highly correlated (low diversity within type), and expensive. Store managers will be moderately accurate (hopefully), highly diverse (owing to experience and regional variation), and inexpensive.

- If your crowd is going to be small, then you should create a crowd of all market researchers. They're more accurate—even though they lack diversity—and they cost a lot.

- If you want to form a crowd of 100 people, you may still only want 3 market researchers because their lack of diversity means that the fourth won't get you much more than the first 3. Plus, they cost a lot, so you might even want to cut back to 2. At the same time, you want lots of store managers because you're only able to tap into their diversity by having a good number of them. With only a handful of store managers, you may get a biased sample.

- As a general rule, the bigger the crowd, the more you value diversity. This is not necessarily an intuitive point, but it is a logical one.

- We could think of this as a single crowd of 100 people containing market researchers and 97 store managers, or we could think of this as 2 crowds—a small crowd of market researchers and a large crowd of store managers. If the 2 crowds agree, we should feel confident in the collective prediction, but if they disagree, it gives us an opportunity to think about why they disagree and to perhaps make an even better prediction as a result.

Important Term

variance: Differences in the value of an attribute (informal). The expected value of the squared error of a random variable (formal).

Suggested Reading

Lamberson and Page, "Optimal Forecasting Groups."

Questions to Consider

1. How can it make sense to attach more weight to accurate prediction but not put all of the weight on the single most accurate prediction?

2. Why do some groups put negative weights on some of their models?

Foxes and Hedgehogs—Can I Be Diverse?
Lecture 7

You have learned that diverse models improve collective predictions—that they make crowds smarter. In this lecture, you will learn that individuals who hold diverse models also make better predictions. The course of your life depends on a handful of key decisions, and all of those decisions require you to make predictions. Perhaps you can get opinions from friends and family members, but if they're not different from you, then they will only be helpful if they are individually very accurate. If you can be diverse all by yourself, however, then you'll be better at making predictions.

Making Predictions with Proper Boxes

- One type of predictive model involves predictions based on categorizations and requires 2 steps: partitioning the set of possibilities (dividing up all of the possibilities into sets or categories) and making predictions for each category. Accurate predictions require correctly doing both of these tasks—creating the proper categories and knowing their contents.

- Robert Quinn and Kim Cameron's model of organizational assessment places cultures in 4 boxes: control, compare, create, and collaborate. These correspond to hierarchies, markets, clans, and adhocracies. By placing your organization in one of those boxes, you're able to better understand its culture and predict what sort of interventions will be successful.

- The Myers-Briggs personality test classifies people into boxes such as INTJ, which represents an introverted, intuitive, thinking, and judging person. Knowledge of a person's Myers-Briggs type might allow you to predict how he or she will respond to stress.

- Categorizations like Myers-Briggs or the organizational assessment model place people and organizations in boxes. Those categorizations have value if the following 2 conditions hold.
  - What's in one box must differ meaningfully from what's in another.
  - You have to be able to evaluate what is in each box with some degree of accuracy.

- Total predictive error = variation in data + error in predicted mean. Total predictive error = methods category error + substance category error. Therefore, total predictive error consists of 4 parts: variation in data in methods category, error in predicted mean for methods category, variation in data in substantive category, and error in predicted mean for substantive category.

- A good predictor will have a small total error. This requires 2 skills: constructing categories with little variation within category and accurately predicting the mean within those categories.

- If you can create the proper boxes, then the total error depends only on the predictive errors within each category. If you can also make the correct prediction within each box, then you can make a perfect prediction.

- When making predictions using boxes, predictive error comes from 2 parts.
  - Choosing the proper boxes: This means creating categories so that the variance within those categories is small. If the variance within categories is small, it means that you have all the high values in one box, all the low values in another, and all the medium values in a third. High variation within categories implies that each box contains a mix of values. A good predictor creates categories that have little variation within them. The more categories that you create, the more that you'll be able to lower the variation within categories. However, you need to create the proper categories.

○ Getting the mean right for each box: Even if you can parse the world into the correct categories, you might not know what's happening within those categories. Knowing the proper boxes means that you know what matters (what's known as discrimination) , and knowing the mean within each box means knowing how things matter (what's known as calibration).

The Many-Model Thinker: Intersecting Boxes

- We now possess a model of how people predict and what would allow someone to predict well, which involves lots of boxes and good predictions within boxes. Suppose that you have one way of looking at the world. That's one set of boxes. Suppose that you have 2 ways of looking at the world. That's 2 sets of boxes. That means that you can take intersections of boxes and create even more boxes.

- Suppose that you are trying to forecast the success of a new restaurant. You might have one model based on the ethnicity of the food. With this model, you might create 6 boxes: American, French, Italian, Korean, Japanese, and Lebanese. Within each box, you can make a prediction. That prediction might be that Japanese and Lebanese restaurants do best, followed by Italian and French.

- You might have a second model based on the prices that they charge for food. In this case, you can create 3 boxes: cheap, moderate, and expensive. If the restaurant will be located in a college town with many students, then inexpensive restaurants might do best. If the town also has many doctors in addition to students, then expensive restaurants might also do well. In this town, moderately priced restaurants do the worst.

- Suppose that the restaurant in question is a cheap Lebanese place. Both models predict that it will do well, so you might conclude that it will do well. Suppose that it's a moderately priced Lebanese restaurant. In that case, your models contradict each other, so you have to make a prediction based on the new box that intersects the Lebanese box and the moderate box—so you might extrapolate between the 2 predictions.

- By having 2 models, you can create more boxes, which is good. If the models are relevant, then they might be proper boxes, or boxes with low variance within them. In addition, because you have many models, you probably have a reasonable way of making predictions within the new boxes. Therefore, your error within those boxes should be lower as well. Thus, you should be able to make good predictions, and you should be able to make better predictions than if you had just one model.

Tetlock's Foxes and Hedgehogs

- Political scientist and management professor Philip Tetlock conducted a study for over a decade in which he coded predictions from hundreds of experts, nonexperts, and students who collectively made tens of thousands of predictions. He found that people with more models are able to create more proper boxes and make better predictions within those boxes. In other words, diverse thinkers predict with greater accuracy.

- Tetlock didn't set out to test whether diverse thinkers outperformed people with a single model; instead, he took a much broader approach. He was asking 2 fundamental questions about our human capabilities: Can experts predict the future? If so, which type of experts? In his book *Expert Political Judgment*, he details the responses to these questions. In response to the first question, he finds that experts cannot predict the future with much accuracy, and for the second, he finds that those who can with any success tend to rely on multiple models.

- The cover of Tetlock's book shows a fox and a hedgehog. These images are borrowed from the political philosopher Isaiah Berlin. In writing about Tolstoy, Berlin borrowed this quote from Archilochus: "The fox knows many things, but the hedgehog knows one big thing." Tetlock found that foxes, people who rely on many models, prove to be more accurate predictors than hedgehogs, people who believe in one big idea.

- Tetlock's first finding was that people proved not very good at predicting. To arrive at that conclusion, Tetlock defined discrimination as corresponding to a low variation within category and calibration as corresponding to accurate prediction of the means within category.

- Tetlock compared the prediction of experts to chimps, which were basically random predictions, and he found that nonexperts didn't do much better than these so-called chimps and that students did worse than chimps.

Making predictions is a pervasive part of your everyday life, and being a diverse individual can help you make better predictions.

- Don't be too dismayed by the lousy performance of people. After all, many events—particularly movements in stock prices—may by their very nature be unpredictable. Some theories state that if you could predict that a stock price would rise, you'd purchase the stock, therefore raising the price until it would no longer rise. This logic underpins the efficient market hypothesis. If that hypothesis is true, stock prices should contain all relevant information, and you should not be able to beat the market. It also means that you could not predict whether a stock will go up or down. If you could, then you'd be able to make money.

- In addition, you can be a little more optimistic when you learn that Tetlock made the chimps pretty smart. For many of his questions, Tetlock asked whether a measure would likely decrease, stay the same, or increase. For example, take the growth rate for the U.S. economy. If GDP growth had been 3% with a **standard deviation** of 1% over the past decade, then Tetlock assumed a **normal distribution** and called any growth rate less than 1/2 of a standard deviation below the mean significant and any growth rate more than 1/2 of a standard deviation above the mean significant.

- If the growth rate really were normally distributed, then 38% of the time it won't change, 31% of the time it will go up, and 31% of the time it will go down. Using this approach, Tetlock constructed a set of boxes that were equally likely to occur. He then assumed that the chimp randomly picked a box. This setup means that the chimp will be right approximately 1/3 of the time.

- People did better than real chimps would have done, but not much better than when dividing the world into 3 categories and randomly picking one. Students did even worse.

- The foxes—people with multiple models—did better than the single-model forecasters. In other words, foxes did better than hedgehogs for 2 main reasons: Foxes take less extreme views, and they respond better to information.

- In reference to the first finding, hedgehogs mostly rely on one big idea. In contrast, foxes see many sides. Some foxes hold optimistic views and other forecast more dire outcomes, but overall, foxes tend to make more conservative forecasts.

- The finding that foxes responded better to information should not be surprising. The more models that you have in your head, the more likely it is that new information will fit within one of your models. A many-model thinker creates more boxes. A single piece of information might have only a small effect on a big box, so it will be ignored—but it can have a big effect on a small box.

- Being a fox doesn't come without costs. Thinking large increases the probability of being illogical. Foxes also contradict themselves. They are more likely to have their predictions violate the laws of probability. The benefit, though, is to be more accurate.

- In light of the fact that diversity makes us better predictors, why don't we all have many models in our heads? It's because it is not easy to seriously engage 2 or more models and think through the nuances of them. It is much easier to resort to thinking about only one model.

Important Terms

normal distribution: The distribution that results from averaging random shocks of finite variance.

standard deviation: The square root of the variance of a random variable. In a normal distribution, 68% of all outcomes lie within 1 standard deviation.

Suggested Reading

Tetlock, *Expert Political Judgment*.

Questions to Consider

1. Explain how creating the right boxes and making the correct predictions within each box contribute to accuracy.

2. What are 2 lessons from Philip Tetlock's work?

Fermi's Barbers—Estimating and Predicting
Lecture 8

In this lecture, you're going to learn 4 methods for how to estimate and predict, including analogies, the Fermi method, linear decomposition, and trend analysis. These methods will put you on a path to being a better predictor. Making predictions is easy, but making accurate predictions is much more difficult. We can rarely foresee the future, but we can—at least at times—place some reasonable bounds on what might transpire. For some problems, 1 of the 4 prediction methods will be more relevant than the others, but for most problems, you will find that multiple methods apply.

A Brief History of Prediction

- For nearly 2000 years, from around 1400 B.C. to A.D. 400, Greeks who wanted to know the future went to the oracle at Delphi. The Greeks considered Delphi to be the navel of the world. Upon visiting the oracle, they would encounter a virtuous older woman known as Pythia, the priestess of Apollo. The oracle wasn't a good predictor, but its failures were chalked up to misinterpretation and not error. Questioning the oracle's veracity came at a huge risk.

- The oracle at Delphi was just one historical method of prediction. Even a partial list inspires awe in the diversity of attempts: astrology, palm reading, tarot cards, the I Ching, the neighing of horses, the patterns of moles on a person's body, and secret codes in sacred texts. Of course, none of these methods has passed scientific scrutiny. Therefore, it is far better to use models, which actually work.

The ancient town known as Delphi is the site of the most important Greek temple and oracle of Apollo.

© Zoonar/Thinkstock.

- Estimation and prediction are 2 separate concepts. To estimate means to make an approximate calculation of some quantity, or amount of value. To predict means to estimate in advance, or to tell the future.

- Predicting is more difficult than estimating because it depends on information that we don't yet know. Predicting is just a type of estimation. Therefore, if we want to learn to predict, we first have to learn to estimate.

Estimation by Analogy

- An analogy is an inference that if 2 things agree on some attributes, then they likely agree on others. To estimate by analogy simply means to find something analogous whose value you do know—or even better, the values of several things—and then to infer the value of the object of interest.

- Suppose that you're asked to estimate the life expectancy of a coyote. To start, you might know that a coyote is a type of dog and that domesticated dogs live between 8 and 15 years. Therefore, you might guess that coyotes live for about the same amount of time.

- Furthermore, you can build from that analogy. A key to using models properly is not to take predictions as fact but to use them as starting points to think. You might think that coyotes are not overbred, so they might live longer than dogs. However, coyotes don't get yearly trips to the veterinarian. As a result, you might then estimate 10-12 years, which is the correct answer.

- Different people draw different analogies—which is good because it leads to different predictions. Analogies can also be helpful in placing boundaries on values.

The Fermi Method

- The Fermi method gets its name from the Italian physicist Enrico Fermi, who was known for making accurate estimates using little or no actual data. Fermi's approach breaks an estimate down into parts and then multiplies those parts together. This technique is now known as dimensional analysis.

- In order to see how different people solved interesting problems, Google used to ask their interviewees: How many golf balls can you put on a school bus? To solve this problem using Fermi's method, we first identify the ratio that we want to solve: $\frac{\text{golf balls}}{\text{school bus}}$.

- We then decompose this ratio into 2 ratios. The first is the number of golf balls per cubic foot, and the second is the number of cubic feet inside a school bus: $\frac{\text{golf balls}}{\text{cubic feet}} \times \frac{\text{cubic feet}}{\text{school bus}}$.

- This now seems like a much more manageable problem. First, we can tackle how may golf balls there are in a square foot. Suppose that golf balls are cubes—which they're

Enrico Fermi (1901–1954) was an Italian physicist who was awarded the 1938 Nobel Prize for Physics.

© National Archives and Records Administration.

not. Golf balls are a little bigger than 1.5 inches in diameter. Given that we have square golf balls, let's make them 1.5 inches on a side. That means that if we packed our square golf balls into a box that is 12 inches on a side, we would get $8 \times 8 \times 8$, or 512 golf balls. To keep the math simple, we can make that an even 500.

- The inside of a school bus is probably about 40 feet long, a little over 6 feet high, and about 8 feet wide. If we multiply 40 by 6, we get 240, which we can round to 250. If we then multiply that by 8 feet, we get 2000 cubic feet.

- To get our final answer, we just multiply 500 (the number of golf balls per cubic foot) by 2000 (the number of cubic feet in a school bus), which equals 1 million. Then, we have to consider the curve of the ceiling and the fact that the seats take up some of the space. Therefore, we might end up with around 750,000, which is probably close to the correct answer.

- The Fermi method will not always work this well, but we can do some leverage diversity to gauge how accurate it will be. As we get a better sense of bounds on our predictions of the parts, we get a good sense of how accurate our prediction is.

Linear Decomposition

- Linear decomposition is a method that relies on decomposing a whole into parts and then adding up those parts. For example, if we wanted to estimate the weight of a house, we could decompose the house into all of its parts, including the wood, bricks, tile, roofing materials, appliances, and furniture. To get an estimate of the weight of a house, we would simply add up our estimates of all the parts.

- This method works well, provided that the following 2 conditions are met.
  - The value of the whole approximately equals the value of the parts.
  - We have to know the value of the parts, or at least be able to make better guesses.

- Suppose that you walk into your favorite local sandwich shop and order a sub. How can you make an estimate of how many calories are in the sub?

- Start by breaking the sub apart. You see a bun, mayo, cheese, tomato and lettuce. Then, you can write a simple linear equation that includes your estimates for all of the parts: sub calories = bun calories (probably 150 calories) + mayo calories (about 100) + cheese calories (about 100) + tomato calories (maybe 10) + lettuce calories (at most 5). Next, add 150 + 100 + 100 + 10 + 5 = 365.

- You can also use the linear attribute model to predict the future. For example, if you wanted to predict how much it would cost to open a coffee shop, you could make a list of prices for all of the components and add them.

Trend Analysis

- A trend prediction relies on what statisticians call a time series, or a sequence of data. Daily temperatures in Barstow, California, can be placed in a time series—as can stock prices, consumer confidence, or the price of cheese. Collecting a time series allows us to make predictions about the future.

- In 1965, Gordon Moore, one of the founders of Intel, noticed that the number of transistors that can be placed on an integrated circuit doubled every 2 years, and doubling implies a pretty fast increase. Since 1965, Moore's law (which is more like an empirical pattern or trend than a law) has basically held.

- Moore's law is an example of an exponential trend. The amount of money you'll have in the bank if you invest m dollars at a rate r also follows an exponential trend. After t years, you'll have $m(1 + r)^t$, which is the formula for exponential growth.

- An example of a linear trend is if your income increases by $2000 per year.

- An example of a cyclical trend is if the weather in a particular state is warm in the summer and cool in the winter.

- A regression to the mean is a random sequence of moves up and down around some mean value. For example, a person's body temperature averages about 98.6 degrees, but it fluctuates.

- Time series are used to predict the future by analyzing their trends.

The Many-Model Thinker

- Each of these methods can work and improve your ability to estimate, but they work best in combination. In general, you can predict better when you use multiple, diverse models.

- Suppose that you're thinking of selling your house and you want to know how much you can sell it for. How do you make such an estimate? The Fermi method and trend analysis probably don't apply, but you might be able to estimate by analogy. You can look at other similar houses in your neighborhood or in similar neighborhoods and see what they sold for recently. In fact, this is part of how banks appraise houses—by looking at what they call comparables.

- To do linear decomposition, you can start by breaking the house into components: house = lot + size in square feet + kitchen quality + number bedrooms + number of bathrooms.

- You need to know the value of each of these parts to make an estimate, but all of these are knowable. This is the other part of how banks appraise home values. After looking at comparables, they add in some linear terms. For example, if your house has a cool sun porch and none of the others do, they add in the value of the sun porch. If your house has a tiny kitchen with avocado appliances, they subtract these undesirable aspects of your kitchen. By combining models, the lender can make a more accurate estimate of your house's value—and so can you.

Practicing Forecasting

- An obvious reason that learning to estimate based on these models is important is that you can't look up the future on the Internet. In addition, as much information as there is, there's still a lot that we cannot find on the Internet—for various reasons.

- Learning how to estimate with the help of these models can also lead to self-improvement. In other words, people improve by building skills through practice—with expert feedback. If you want to be able to predict the future, you need practice, and you can practice by estimating—for example, the number of bricks in the Great Wall of China—and then verifying your answer on the web. Your answers won't often be exactly correct, but they'll sometimes be close.

Questions to Consider

1. Describe 3 ways that you could estimate the value of a business.

2. How many tortilla chips could you fit inside the Washington Monument?

Problem Solving
Lecture 9

In this lecture, and in the 5 that follow, you will learn about problem solving—how individuals, teams, and groups find better solutions to problems and innovate. The goal of this lecture is to introduce you to a general problem-solving framework that will be used in the next few lectures and that relies on perspectives and heuristics. Using that model, you will observe how talent (the number of tools) and diversity (different tools) matter and how a person's value to a team depends on how that person's tools complement the tools of others.

Solving Problems

- Our ability to solve problems plays the central role in our continued collective prosperity. Meeting some of the big challenges that we face as a society—including reducing poverty, improving education, managing the environment, preventing financial catastrophes, and understanding our genetic code—requires us to solve problems. We're trying to meet those challenges, which is why more and more people are classified as problem solvers.

- Problem solving differs from prediction. Just because diversity proves useful in prediction does not mean that it will be useful in problem solving. In fact, some forms of diversity harm problem solving. For example, on the plus side, language diversity lends richness to the human experience, but it also has detrimental effects. It slows communication and increases the likelihood of miscommunication.

- Prediction requires figuring out some future or unknown state of the world or value. In contrast, problem solving consists of finding better solutions to problems—such as building a more efficient combustion engine or a more useful search algorithm for the Internet.

- Because problem solving differs from prediction, the types of diversity relevant to problem solving will differ from the types relevant to prediction. With predictions, we combine diverse models. With problem solving, we also combine, but there's a fundamental difference in how we combine. With predictions, we average. With ideas, we mash up. We can also choose not to combine. Sometimes ideas point us in opposite directions; then, we have to choose one.

- The fact that we don't have to combine means that we can include even more outside-the-box ideas. A crazy prediction that is far from the actual value will make the collective prediction less accurate. Such predictions, and the people who make them, hurt the crowd. With problem solving, however, we can toss aside an idea that doesn't work, or we can think about it for a minute because perhaps it might spark a related idea that does make sense.

Problem Solving: Production of Ideas

- Think about problem solving as the production of new ideas. Each idea will have a value associated with it—with better ideas having higher values.

- Imagine that a small group of professors is tasked with planning a 2-day trip to Rome for a group of alumni and organize a meeting to discuss the itinerary. Imagine that each person in the group comes to the meeting with an itinerary in mind. To avoid complicating the model, assume that there is a leader of the group who evaluates each itinerary and then selects the best.

- In this primitive model of problem solving, the value of the group equals the value of the best person in the group. No communication occurs, and there is no sharing of ideas. As a result, there are no synergies from diversity or talent.

- Suppose that someone's ability to create a good itinerary correlated perfectly with his or her travel planner talent level. Suppose also that the leader knew these talent levels. If so, the leader would have no need for the group because he or she could just ask the person with the most talent for the best itinerary.

- If the leader doesn't know how much talent each person has, then we can think of each person's talent as a draw from a normal distribution, a **bell curve**. If the leader only asks one person to make up an itinerary, he or she gets just one draw. On average, this will be near the average. As the leader gets itineraries from more people, he or she is more likely to get one near the right tail (the good side) of the distribution—in addition to one near the left (bad) tail, but she can disregard that one.

- Thus, in this model of problem solving, groups outperform individuals, and they do so because a group more likely includes someone of high talent. However, this model still leaves out any group dynamics—any interactions between the ideas and thoughts of the participants.

- Keep in mind that one cannot see all of Rome in 2 days, so these itineraries will involve some tough choices. Suppose that the best proposed itinerary was submitted by a historian and that he structures the days by historical era. Suppose that an operations research professor submitted the lowest valued itinerary and that she specializes in finding minimal routes between locations. Her itinerary took a list of attractions that she liked and found a minimal route. This itinerary had the shortest walking distance, but it was thought by the leader to produce too much cognitive dissonance because the alumni would be jumping from era to era.

- The idea from the operations research professor can improve upon the best idea. The operations researcher's route may not be good, but her tools are. If we ask the operations researcher to employ some of her route-minimizing tools, she would probably propose a few improvements to the historian's route.

- This example demonstrates how solutions can be combined to form even better solutions and why problem solving consists of more than just choosing the best solution. The example also reveals the 2 features of problem solving that will be the focus of the next 5 lectures of this course: perspectives and heuristics.

Perspectives and Heuristics

- A perspective is a representation of the set of solutions to a problem. The historian's perspective considered each attraction according to its place in history. We can think of taking a list of the most important attractions in Rome and assigning to each a date. This historical ordering is her perspective. The operations research professor had a different perspective. She listed the same attractions by their locations on a map—not caring about their historical placement. This provides a different perspective.

- Given a perspective, an individual needs some way of finding good solutions: tricks, recipes, algorithms, and rules of thumb. These are heuristics. The historian's heuristics probably involved constructing a route that produced a consistent narrative. Attractions that involved the same historical actors or eras would be more likely to be considered in sequence. The operations researcher's heuristics would be more algorithmic—such as switching pairs of attractions to see if the route becomes shorter.

- Combining the 2 ideas created a better solution. We took the best solution, the historian's solution, and reimagined it in the operation researcher's perspective. We then applied one of the operations researcher's heuristics—switching pairs of attractions—to locate a better solution.

- These 2 ideas provide the foundation for much of what's to follow in the next 5 lectures: Diverse perspectives enable people to see solutions differently, and diverse heuristics enable people to locate new and better solutions.

- When we think of people as having perspectives and heuristics, ability becomes contingent on who else is working on a problem. Anyone's value in a problem-solving context depends on coming up with something new. If he or she doesn't have anything new to add—any new perspectives or heuristics—he or she won't improve the value of the solution. It's not that the person is not smart or that he or she doesn't have ability. It's just that we already have someone who knows what he or she knows.

The Toolbox Model

- We can think of each person in a group as a collection of tools. Formally, these will be perspectives and heuristics, but we can metaphorically think of them as tools to make the core logic as transparent as possible.

- Each of the people that you hire brings with him or her a toolbox. On the job, they may learn even more tools, but for the moment, assume that these toolboxes remained fixed. With this simple metaphorical model, we can draw some rather surprising insights.

- First, a person's contribution depends on the number of tools and their diversity relative to those of other team members. In this model, talent, ability, skill, or intelligence will be captured by the number of tools that a person possesses. Someone who has more tools will be more likely to possess one that works on the problem. With everything else being equal, someone with more tools will be more likely to find an improvement or make an innovation.

- Second, diversity relative to the team also matters. For example, within a group of 10 problem solvers, 2 people possess lots of matrix algebra skills and one knows about networks, both of which are relevant to the hypothetical software problem that you are having. The first 2 people both have many tools, but they have the same tools. The third person has fewer tools (less ability), but they are different tools, so that means that the added value of the third person will probably be higher.

- If we think about talent as tools, a person's contribution depends on what different and relevant tools he or she brings. There exist 2 ways to have different tools: to have more tools or to have different tools. Of course, all of these tools have to be relevant.

- Someone's contribution will also be contingent on when he or she works on the problem. We see this in stark form when 2 people have the same tools. Whomever goes first looks great—perhaps even like a genius—and whomever goes second adds no value.

- Suppose that people have toolboxes consisting of perspectives and heuristics and that each, if given the problem on his or her own, would do equally well—that is, they have the same talent level. Even with that restriction, the contribution of each person can be any amount you want. In practice, if you have more tools, you're also more likely to have unique tools, and you'll be more likely to make a contribution—to improve the existing value of a solution. However, you can have less valuable tools and still add value.

- Heuristics travel. A tool that we learn for one problem may work for another. It may not, but it could. Applying heuristics to new problems—combination and **recombination**—drives innovation, which is a big part of economic growth. Perspectives also travel. We can take a perspective that we've learned about in one context and apply it in another context.

Important Terms

bell curve: A normal curve, or distribution.

recombination: The combining of existing ideas and technologies to create new ideas and technologies.

Suggested Reading

Hong and Page, "Problem Solving by Heterogeneous Agents."

Page, *The Difference*, chap. 6.

Questions to Consider

1. How does problem solving differ from prediction?

2. What are a few of the insights that can be drawn from the toolbox model?

Diverse Perspectives
Lecture 10

In the previous lecture, you discovered how problem solving relies on perspectives and heuristics. In this lecture, your focus is going to be on perspectives, which are representations or encodings of problems. In some cases, diverse perspectives take something difficult and make it simple, and the result is transcendent. Another mechanism of diverse perspectives is to enlarge the set of points that people consider. The innovation writer Steven Johnson calls these other possible solutions "the adjacent possible." Demonstrating these 2 benefits of perspectives—making the obtuse transparent and enlarging the set of the possible—is the focus of this lecture.

Diversity and Transcendence

- Diverse perspectives provide the foundations for breakthroughs and innovations. Diverse perspectives seem to be transcendent—as though they were handed down by some mysterious, all-knowing higher authority. A new perspective can bring order and simplicity to what once seemed to be a complex morass.

- Unlike some of the other great geniuses—Newton, Gauss, Feynman, or Gell-Mann—Albert Einstein was not tagged early on as exceedingly special. He was a top-notch student (not the apocryphal C student we're sometimes told) and an even better physicist.

- Einstein had a gift for seeing the physical world through new perspectives. Einstein won the Nobel Prize for his work on the photoelectric effect. Einstein's idea was to see light as consisting of tiny particles, or quanta, as opposed to thinking of light as a continuous wave. It was an entirely new perspective, and it led to many breakthroughs—including the laser.

- In other words, Einstein saw light in a way that was different from how anyone else had ever seen it. His more famous discovery was his theory of relativity, which involves the notion of curved space-time. Again, Einstein saw reality in a new way, and in doing so, created order where none had been. In each case, Einstein was introducing a new perspective—a new way of thinking about a phenomenon.

Sum to 15

- Herbert Simon, a Nobel Prize winner in Economics, developed a game called sum to 15. In this 2-player game, 9 cards numbered from 1 to 9 are laid in a row on a table. One player is randomly selected to go first. Each player then takes turns selecting cards. The first player to have in his or her hand exactly 3 cards that sum to 15 wins. If after all 9 cards have been selected no one has some set of 3 cards in his or her hand that adds up to fifteen, the game is a tie. The final rule is that you only get 5 seconds to pick a card.

- At some point in math class, you probably learned about magic squares. In a magic square, every column, row, and diagonal sums to 15. The following is an example.

6	1	8
7	5	3
2	9	4

- We can use the magic square as an alternative perspective, or transcendent perspective, on this game. Basically, sum to 15 is tic-tac-toe—but, it's tic-tac-toe in a different perspective. However, it's the wrong perspective, which is why sum to 15 is difficult and tic-tac-toe is easy.

- This possibility for transcendence, the possibility of turning a complicated reality into tic-tac-toe, is one big reason why businesses, nonprofits, universities, governments, high schools, and even religious organizations sing the praises of diverse perspectives. Sadly, though, finding these transcendent perspectives takes effort, devotion, luck—and even genius.

The Adjacent Possible

- The second equally important—though less sublime—value of diverse perspectives is enlarging the adjacent possible. To introduce and formalize the idea of the adjacent possible, we need to start with a concept developed by ecologist Sewall Wright that is called a fitness landscape.

- Think of the problem of creating a living thing. For example, a turtle has DNA that consists of genes and a whole bunch of stuff between those genes that we don't yet fully understand. Those genes produce proteins and differentiated cells and, eventually, a turtle. If we change a gene, then we may change the resulting turtle.

- To compare this new turtle with other turtles, Wright assigns to each a "fitness," which can be loosely defined as the ability of the turtle to reproduce. We can then create a landscape by putting the genetic type on the x-axis and fitness on the y-axis. That landscape will generally be considered to be a **rugged landscape**.

- DNA consists of nucleotides. Each nucleotide has 1 of 4 bases: adenine (A), cytosine (C), guanine (G), or thymine (T). Each strand of DNA can be represented by a long string of As, Cs, Ts and Gs. Humans and turtles are diploid (2 strands), some trout are triploid (3 strands), and durum wheat is tetraploid (4 strands).

- Let's simplify and assume that instead of 4 bases, there are only 2—which we'll call A and B. We'll also assume that the organism we're evolving has a single strand of DNA. Biologists call such organisms—including bees, ants, and wasps—haploid.

- In this example, the DNA is a long string of As and Bs. Let's say that it is of length 100. The adjacent possible depends on what our heuristics are. Let's suppose that our only heuristic is to switch As for Bs. Biologists call this a one-bit mutation. That means that any one of our As could get switched to a B, or any one of our Bs could get switched to an A—that there exist exactly 100 strings that are a one-bit mutation away. These 100 neighboring strings are the adjacent possible.

- Let's see how a new perspective can change the set of the adjacent possible. Suppose that we break the string of length 100 into 50 pairs of 2 and that we represent each pair using the following perspective: First, we write down the first letter in the pair—for example, AB and AA will both get an A, and BA and BB will both get a B—and then we write an S if the second letter is the same as the first and a D if the second letter is different. In this way, AA becomes AS, AB becomes AD, BA becomes BD, and BB becomes BS.

- Let's again assume that our only heuristic is one-bit mutation. We now will assume that mutation can also switch Ds and Ss. Let's take a string of length 4 in the original perspective: AABA. Its adjacent possible consists of BABA, ABBA, AAAA, and AABB. In our new perspective, AABA becomes ASBD. After a one-bit mutation, we also get 4 new strings: BSBD or BBBA, ADBD or ABBA, ASAD or AAAB, and ASBS or AABB. Notice that 2 of them—AABB and ABBA—are the same, but 2 differ. These are new members of the adjacent possible.

- If 2 people encode the same problem differently—if they each use a different perspective—then solutions that are near or adjacent in one perspective may be a long way away from the other perspective. Therefore, what seems obvious (or adjacent) to one person may seem like a novel idea to another, and what seems like a pedestrian one-bit mutation to one person may seem like a brilliant, unexpected idea to another.

- This expansion of the adjacent possible by bringing in new people is one way to promote thinking outside of the box. In fact, if we think of the box as the set of possible solutions, a new perspective doesn't really generate thinking outside of the box. Instead, it's more like reorganizing the box, and that reorganization brings near some things that used to be far away.

- When people come up with new ideas, they often start from solutions that other people have found. Then, they apply their own perspectives to the problems, and by expanding the set of the adjacent possible, they find new solutions. If people have different adjacent possibles, then they propose different ideas. Diverse groups think of more new ideas because they have more adjacent possibles.

Transcendent Landscapes

- Suppose that you are a modern-day Willy Wonka and that you are trying to come up with a new candy bar. Your confectioners develop a machine that can make any one of 5000 varieties. Your job, as owner and official taster, is to find the best one. First, you need a perspective—some way to represent all of those different varieties.

- If you take a 1-dimensional perspective and arrange the candy bars in a single line, then you could list any one of the 5000 candy bars first, any one of 4999 candy bars second, and so on. Therefore, the total number equals $5000 \times 4999 \times 4998 \times \ldots$. Mathematicians call this 5000 factorial (5000!), or $4.28 \times 10^{16,326}$, which is 4 followed by over 16,000 zeros.

- Remembering Sewall Wright's landscape, suppose that each candy bar (if you had the time to taste them all) would get a score between 0 and 100—with higher scores being better. A good perspective would create order. For example, label the worst candy bar with the number 1, the second worst with the number 2, and so on until the best candy bar gets the value 5000.

- If we draw this landscape, we get one big slope leading upward. On this landscape, if we searched by looking to the left and right, we would always find our way to the best candy bar. This landscape makes the problem simple. Alternatively, we could put the best candy bar at 1 and the worst at 5000. This, too, would be a transcendent landscape.

- There are other transcendent landscapes as well. We could place the best bar at any number—1245, for example—and then create a single peak by arranging the bars so that the other best bars are near the peak and the worst bars are at the extremes. These single-peaked landscapes are called Mount Fuji landscapes. On a Mount Fuji landscape, if you are not at the optimum, then 1 of the 2 neighboring bars—one of the adjacent possible—will be an improvement. One direction always goes up.

- There exist billions of Mount Fuji landscapes, but there exist $10^{16,000}$ landscapes. Most landscapes are random; they create no structure. That's the problem—they have thousands of peaks. On a random landscape, your adjacent possible will be random. Therefore, once a good solution has been found, if you pick 2 random solutions, they likely won't be better. In the real world, this means that if you already have a good solution and you bring in a random perspective, then it probably won't help.

- As we gain expertise, as we develop a richer set of experiences, and as we learn more diverse ways of thinking, we become better at coming up with new perspectives.

- Perspectives can sometimes travel. They can be used for other purposes. Biologists call this exaptation, in which something evolved for one purpose and finds some other purpose for which it is better suited. The feathers on a bird represent the classic example. Scientific evidence suggests that feathers evolved for temperature regulation, but a few mutations later, they led to flight.

rugged landscape: A graphical representation of a difficult problem in which the value of a potential solution is represented as an elevation.

Suggested Reading

Page, *The Difference*, chap. 1.

Questions to Consider

1. Give 2 perspectives for all of the houses on your street.

2. Why do better perspectives have fewer peaks?

Heuristics and the Adjacent Possible
Lecture 11

O nce someone has a perspective on a problem, he or she tries to find improvements within that perspective through the use of heuristics. This lecture introduces some rudimentary heuristics and shows how diverse heuristics expand the adjacent possible. It also demonstrates the 2 ways that heuristics produce outside-the-box thinking. In this lecture, you will learn about 2 sophisticated computational heuristics—simulated annealing and drowning ants—and you will see how organizations and societies use similar heuristics. Whether in the minds of people or in computer code, heuristics enable us to find better solutions to problems.

Simple, Local Heuristics

- Simple heuristics are sometimes called local heuristics, which introduce a new solution that's near to—or in the neighborhood of—the existing solutions.

- For example, suppose that you own a business that makes small wooden coasters for coffee cups. These coasters entail gluing together small leftover pieces of wood cut to size. Your process could currently proceed as follows: cut, glue, sand, varnish. However, you could switch the order to cut, sand, glue, varnish, and you might find that this new order saves you time and money because in the past, the sanding might have had to wait until the glue dried. Note, though, that not all orders would make sense.

- This simple switching algorithm, which is an example of a local heuristic, can be applied to any problems for which the solution can be written as an ordered list. Another example of a local heuristic is a greedy algorithm, which looks at solutions near the current point and chooses the one that is best. It then looks at all the points near that new point and chooses the best among those.

- For example, suppose that you're on a rugged landscape at the bottom of a hill and there exist 2 directions up: either left or right. Perhaps the left direction is steeper. A greedy heuristic would go left.

- Greedy algorithms can be contrasted with improving algorithms, which move to a new solution if it is better but does not necessarily move to the best solution nearby. One reason to not be greedy is that it takes too much time. If you can find an improvement, take it. By the time you've proven that an option is the best, you might already have climbed even further through a series of improvements.

- Furthermore, suppose that the current solution lies in a valley between 2 hills, one of which exceeds the other in height. The greedy algorithm would climb whichever hill is steeper at the base—but would have no guarantee that the steeper hill is taller. In other words, what's locally best does not need to be part of the best solution.

Outside-the-Box Thinking

- Assume that the solution to a problem has multiple dimensions or attributes. We can write the status-quo solution as a vector $(x_1, x_2, \ldots, x_n)$. A local heuristic changes only a small number of those attributes and typically changes them only a little bit. Making small changes attribute by attribute would be the canonical local heuristic.

- We can use this simple mathematical formalism to describe 2 types of outside-the-box thinking. Each relies on a different construction of the box.

- Suppose that you own a jelly company and that you're trying to improve the sales of your grape jelly. Your current product can be thought of as a list of attributes—such as sugar content and chunkiness—or as a recipe, an ordered list of instructions for making the jam.

- Suppose that some people in the company are thinking about how to make small changes to the product to improve its taste or marketability and that someone suggests making it green (because grapes are green). This idea is only out of the box if you ruled out changing the color of the jam. If so, then the "box" in which people were thinking did not contain green jam. More likely, color may only have been off limits because people stopped thinking about it, forgetting that they could change it. As a result, if someone thinks about changing it, then he or she seems very innovative.

- The other type of outside-the-box heuristic relies on nonlocal heuristics, which jump outside of what people think is reasonable. Perhaps the most famous long-leap heuristic is referred to as the do-the-opposite heuristic, in which people do the opposite of the current solution—not on every attribute, but on some attribute or subset of attributes.

- For example, normally, hotels tell us how much we will have to pay to spend the night, and we can accept or refuse the offer. However, with the online hotel-booking company called Priceline, the opposite occurs. People tell the hotel how much they are willing to pay, and the hotel can accept or refuse the offer.

Professions and Heuristics
- Within any profession, there exist a vast collection of heuristics. Engineers, plumbers, hair stylists, nuclear physicists, and dog trainers all develop heuristics to fit the problems they confront. For example, mathematicians use heuristics to solve problems, and one such heuristic is adding 0, which operates on the basis that any number plus 0 equals 0.

- Consider the following expression: $x^4 + 4x^3 + 6x^2 + 4x + 6$. Adding a specific form of 0—negative 5 plus 5—results in $x^4 + 4x^3 + 6x^2 + 4x + 6 - 5 + 5$. Then, the expression can be written as $x^4 + 4x^3 + 6x^2 + 4x + 1 + 5$, which equals $(x + 1)^4 + 5$—a much simpler expression.

- Heuristics don't always transfer to new domains, though they sometimes do, and when they do, they are another form of exaptation. With heuristics, exaptation occurs when a heuristic that was developed for one purpose is applied for another. Many innovations arise through exaptation. Therefore, one way to be good at innovating is to interact with people who are different from you—who have developed different tricks.

Sophisticated Heuristics

- Think again about local and greedy heuristics and climbing on rugged landscapes. Either type of heuristic will get stuck on small hills. Think of a rugged landscape with lots of peaks. A greedy search algorithm will just climb each little peak and get stuck—which is not very effective. It would be better if we could somehow smooth out those peaks. One way to smooth the peaks relies on allowing errors, which is the basic idea behind **simulated annealing**.

- For each possible solution x, define a neighborhood of solutions. These are solutions that are close to x that are within the box. Given a solution x, choose some random point in the neighborhood, applying 2 rules: If the new solution is better, move there, and if the new solution is worse, move there with some probability p. This probability p depends on 2 factors: how much worse the new solution is, which is called loss, and a parameter called the temperature.

- The bigger the loss, the less likely we move to the new solution—which makes sense because we wouldn't want to move to a terrible solution, but we might be willing to move to a solution that's only slightly worse. By accepting small mistakes, we might be able to climb over a little hillock on our landscape. By going down a little bit, we might then be able to go up even higher. At some point, we'd like to stop accepting any solution that is worse and settle on top of a hill, which is where temperature comes in.

- This heuristic, which computer scientists and statisticians use on a variety of problems, mimics real annealing, which is the heating up and cooling down of metals and glasses to get ordered structures. In the process of annealing, when temperatures are high, molecules are dancing all over the place. In a simulated annealing algorithm, high temperatures mean that you are more likely to accept mistakes and even bigger mistakes. As you anneal the temperature, or cool it, you're less likely to accept mistakes.

- To make this formal, computer scientists have an annealing schedule that tells us how quickly to cool. They also use a mathematical expression that gives the probability of accepting an error. Let "loss" denote the decrease in value and "temp" denote the temperature. The probability of accepting a new solution with a value that is lower by the amount "loss" equals $\frac{1}{e^{\text{loss/temp}}}$. The e in this expression is known as Euler's constant, and it is equal to 2.71828.

- If loss is large relative to temp, this equals 1 divided by e raised to a huge power, so that's effectively 0. However, when temp is large relative to loss, we get 1 divided by e to the 0th power, which equals one. Therefore, when the loss is big and the temp is low, we don't accept the new point. When the loss is low and the temp is high, we do.

- In the process of annealing, we start out with a high temperature, which allows us to move about the space of solutions pretty quickly. We always take improvements, and we often accept losses, but we're less likely to take huge losses. We then slowly cool the process, which means that we accept fewer and fewer losses. We let the temperature get colder and colder—until it's eventually 0. At 0 temperature, the heuristic becomes local, improving the search, and eventually we stop. The annealing, or cooling, schedule gives us the rate that we let the temperature fall, and different types of problems use different cooling schedules.

- Another sophisticated heuristic is an example of a population heuristic called drowning ants. It is a population heuristic because instead of iteratively improving one solution, we start with a population of heuristics and simultaneously look for improvements.

- With this heuristic, you randomly guess a bunch of solutions. You then apply a locally improving heuristic at each of those solutions. Metaphorically, think of each of those locally improving heuristics as a small hill-climbing ant on a rugged landscape. Then, imagine a flood. As soon as an ant's feet get wet, assume that it sends an alarm and gets rescued by a boat. Over time, as the floodwaters rise, fewer and fewer ants will be left on the landscape. Eventually, only one ant will be left. This will be the solution that the heuristic gives.

Heuristics and Humans

- Simulated annealing and drowning ants can be organizational and institutional heuristics—routines followed by groups of people within an organization or even by an entire society to locate better solutions to a problem.

- For example, the brainstorming process that is so common to organizations is exapted annealing. In addition, market forces act similar to the drowning ants algorithm. Partly for this reason, for many problems, market forces result in good solutions. Note that if we don't start out with a lot of ants, then we typically won't find as good a solution to our problem.

- In addition to humans, computers use heuristics—and they are probably better at using them than we are. Even though heuristics can be taught to computers, it does not mean that eventually we will become obsolete because many of our problems are based on the essence of who we are, and computers won't know that.

simulated annealing: A search algorithm in which the probability of making an error decreases over time.

Page, *The Difference*, chap. 2.

1. Describe 2 similarities and 1 difference between simulated annealing and brainstorming.

2. Think of an example in which the do-the-opposite heuristic has worked in your own life.

Diversity Trumps Ability
Lecture 12

In this lecture, you will encounter problem solving in a broader context than the way in which it has been discussed in previous lectures due to the addressing of both perspectives and heuristics. The goal of this lecture is to introduce you to a theorem that shows that often, when putting together a team, diversity trumps ability. In other words, you'd rather have diverse members than homogeneous members. However, you will discover some conditions that must hold in order for the theorem to be true. This theorem will allow you to begin to understand when and how cognitive diversity enables people to find better solutions to problems.

Local and Global Optima

- A problem-solving model has 2 parts: a problem and problem solvers. The problem consists of a domain, a set of possible solutions, and an objective function, a function that assigns a value to each solution.

- Suppose that we're trying to improve the fuel efficiency of an automobile. The solution space consists of all possible car designs within some constraint set. For example, if we're working on a minivan, then we cannot turn it into a subcompact. The domain of the problem, s, is the set of solutions. Think of s as a large, finite set: $s_1, s_2, \ldots, s_n$. We can use set notation to write these solutions as $\{s_1, s_2, \ldots, s_n\}$.

- The objective function, f, assigns to each solution a value. Note that the function value is the same for everyone and is easily computed. For example, if someone proposes solution s_{17}, then we just plug it into our formula and get the value $f(s_{17})$. The assumptions that the function is the same for everyone and easily computed are strong assumptions, and they often fail to hold in real-world applications.

- For engineering problems, the assumptions will typically hold. Most engineering problems will be well defined, and we can test the proposed solutions. For example, if the problem is to find the lightest metal that will withstand a given force, any candidate solution can be weighed and tested. For other problems, such as coming up with an advertising campaign or a tax code, even if we agree on our objective—to sell a product or raise a given amount of revenue—we may not have an easy way to evaluate outcomes.

- Each problem solver has a perspective on the problem—that is, some representation of all the solutions. Each problem solver also has a set of heuristics that he or she applies to his or her encoding. Thus, given some solution, a problem solver can represent it in his or her perspective and then apply his or her heuristics.

- For example, suppose that our best current solution, s_{24}, has a value of 65. Assume that all values lie between 0 and 100. The top problem solver might use a perspective that lines up the designs by numbers and then check the models on either side. This person would then check models s_{23} and s_{25}. If either of those had a higher value, then he or she would propose it, and it would become the new best solution. The second problem solver may have arranged the cars in a network, and his or her weights would be s_1, s_2, and s_5. This is a different perspective. A third problem solver might use the same perspective as the first person but would look 2 to the left and 10 to the right, so he or she would consider s_2 and s_6. Each of these 3 problem solvers has a different set of adjacent possibilities.

- Given a car design— s_{24}, for example—and a problem solver, there will be 2 possible outcomes: The problem solver applies his or her perspective and heuristics and finds something better, or he or she doesn't. If the problem solver doesn't find anything better, then he or she is stuck. The design at which he or she gets stuck is called a **local optimum**.

- The very best solution, what is called the **global optimum**, has to be a local optimum for every problem solver. No one could possibly apply their perspective and heuristics and find a better solution than the best possible solution. Therefore, the global optimum is always a local optimum.

- The notion of local optimum aligns with the rugged landscape representation from a previous lecture. If people use only local or greedy heuristics, then the peaks on the landscape will be the local optima. If they use more sophisticated heuristics, then they may be able to escape some of those local peaks.

- People with better perspectives (landscapes with fewer peaks) and more heuristics (more ways to escape those peaks) will have fewer local optima. As a result, they will, on average, locate better solutions to the problem because they get stuck in fewer places— they have fewer local optima.

- You have just been introduced to a third way to think about problem solvers. First, we thought of them as having abilities, or how well they do on a problem. Then, we thought of them as having tools, or perspectives and heuristics. Now, we can also think of a problem solver by his or her set of local optima. Higher-ability problem solvers tend to have more and better tools and, as a result, have fewer and higher-valued local optima.

- Consider a team of people assigned to a problem. If we want to know how well the team will perform, we need to think about where the team can get stuck. The team can only get stuck if every member of the team gets stuck. Therefore, the only points at which the entire team can get stuck belong to the intersection of their local optima.

When Does Diversity Trump Ability?
- Diversity will trump ability when the diverse group has less overlap in their local optima than the high-ability group. Of course, this won't always be true, but there are 4 conditions that must hold for diversity to trump ability.

The problem must be difficult.

○ For our result to hold, the group of high ability has to have overlap in their local optima. This won't be true if the problem isn't hard; on easy problems, someone will be able to solve it. In general, the harder the problem, the more local optima for everyone, and the worse the high-ability group will do.

The diverse people have to be smart.

○ This is called the calculus condition, and what it amounts to is that the members of the diverse group have to have perspectives that put some structure on the problem. They also have to be able to locate peaks on their landscapes, and they could do this with local or greedy search heuristics. This is called the calculus condition because if you know calculus, you can take derivatives and find points with 0 slope, which include all of the peaks.

You have to be drawing from a large, diverse pool.

○ This condition is subtle, and it has 2 parts. First, we need a large pool because the larger the pool gets, the less diverse the very best problem solvers will be. For example, if you were to go to a small town asking for advice on how to landscape your yard, you might find that the most able people are a landscaper architect, a doctor, and a third-grade art teacher. They'll be diverse. Instead, if you were choosing from residents of New York City, the 3 most able people would all be professional landscape architects. The bigger the pool, the more similar those at the top will be.

○ In addition, the pool has to be diverse. If you're choosing from a large set of people, all of whom have been educated in the same limited set of tools, you're better off choosing the best because they'll have more of those tools, so their local optima will be a subset of the local optima of the others.

The group cannot be too big or too small.

- ○ This last condition is one of those technical conditions that must hold or the logic wouldn't make sense. What's too small? One. By definition, the best person will be better than a random person. What's too big? If you take the entire group, the random group and the group of the best will be identical. Therefore, the diverse group won't be better.

- ○ The diverse group will do better when the groups are big enough that the diversity outweighs the ability of the best but not so big that the group of the best is also diverse.

- In other words, we should expect diversity to be able to trump ability when the problem is hard, when the diverse people have germane tools, when we're drawing from a large, diverse pool, and we actually have a team—as opposed to one person or the whole group.

- Some people jump to the conclusion that we should always have a diverse team, but that's not necessarily true. The amount of diversity needed to tackle a problem depends on the problem. The theorem that explains that diversity will trump ability—called the **diversity trumps ability theorem**—has conditions, and it only tells us when we should expect diversity to triumph.

- There are some implicit assumptions associated with this model. We assumed that there were no communication problems. That was true because we had some method for evaluating solutions. If we don't have that, then the diverse group could have difficulty sharing their novel ideas. In addition, we assumed that there was no cost to trying a new solution. That won't always be true either.

Opposite Proverbs Revisited

- Communication costs and errors partly explain why some people like to say that too many cooks spoil the broth. Cooking broth is irreversible. Suppose that your friend is making some vegetable broth to make a vegetarian minestrone for some other vegetarian friends. If you walk into the kitchen, taste the broth, lament its weakness, and add some chicken stock, the miscommunication between you and your friend leads to an error—and the error is irreversible. There is no way of straining out the chicken from the stock, so you ruined dinner.

- Too many cooks really do spoil the broth. It's not just cooks and broth; many things are sequential and largely irreversible, so it's important to stick with the plan. It's the same reason that military strategists insist upon having a single leader in a battle: Too many generals ruin the battle.

- Of course, none of this implies that too many cooks spoil the menu—they don't. Chefs often collaborate on dishes, and they often apply their unique perspectives and heuristics on the dishes of others.

Important Terms

diversity trumps ability theorem: In problem solving, groups of diverse problem solvers can outperform groups consisting of the best individuals.

global optimum: The best solution to a problem.

local optimum: A peak on a rugged landscape.

Suggested Reading

Hong and Page, "Groups of Diverse Problem Solvers."

Page, *The Difference*, chap. 6.

1. What conditions must hold for diversity to trump ability in problem solving?

2. When would too many cooks spoil the broth?

Digging Holes and Splicing Genes
Lecture 13

The diversity prediction theorem states that collective accuracy depends in equal measure on individual accuracy and collective diversity. In the context of problem solving and innovation, diversity can be even more important than ability—provided, of course, that we are faced with a hard problem, a group of smart problem solvers, a diverse pool from which to choose, and a group that is a moderate size. In this lecture, you will learn what the theoretical results about the value of diversity mean for real groups with real people. In addition, you will discover how our new ways of thinking about diversity help build better teams.

Hole Digging

- In the following model, the act of hole digging will be used as a placeholder for work done by an individual in a production economy. This could include any physical labor, including wood chopping, manufacturing, or farm labor.

- These jobs require hard work, but they also require intelligence. People who spend their lives building cars or houses or working on a farm bring perspectives and heuristics to their work. However, for the purposes of making a point, assume that most of the work—and most of the value of that work—results from getting stuff done and not from solving problems.

- Suppose that you run a hold-digging company that is located in the Midwest, and therefore, hole digging by shovel is a seasonal activity that can only be conducted in the summer.

- Each summer, you need to hire a dozen shovelers. Hundreds of applicants send resumes, but you only care whether they can dig holes—how big and how fast.

- Suppose that you charge your customers $20 per hole and that you pay your workers $10 per hole—a 50/50 split. In that way, over the course of a summer, you make $10 for every hole that's dug, as do your workers. Your interest as a profit-maximizing business owner is to maximize the total number of holes that your workers dig.

- If you have a dozen employees, then your total profit is just $10 times the sum of the number of holes that they dig. Let h_1 denote the number of holes dug by worker number 1, h_2 denote the number dug by worker number 2, and so on. Your profit can be expressed as 10 times $h_1 + h_2 + h_3 + \ldots h_{12}$. Profit $= 10(h_1 + h_2 + h_3 \ldots + h_{12})$.

- You want to hire the 12 individuals who are best at digging holes. To be more specific, if you want to make the most money, then you should have each of your applicants dig holes for an hour and, assuming that you can infer their productivity accurately, hire the best.

- In this environment, you should hire based on talent and not based on diversity. You shouldn't care about perspectives, heuristics, mental models, identity, or ethnicity. By moral, legal, and efficiency grounds, you should not discriminate, but by basic logic, you should also not seek out diversity for the sake of synergies.

- There is no diversity bonus. Now, there could be a small bonus in that someone might figure out a slightly better way to hold the shovel, but that's not likely. Because there's no diversity bonus, there's no need for restructuring.

Gene Splicing

- Let's contrast hole digging with gene splicing. Think of a long strand of DNA, which is a string of nucleotides. DNA is cut using chemicals called restriction enzymes. Each enzyme—and there are thousands of them—identifies a particular sequence of nucleotides. Upon encountering it, the enzyme grabs that sequence of one strand of the DNA and runs off with it, leaving most of the DNA unchanged. This process creates 2 opportunities.

○ The first opportunity is to add on. The DNA now has a small dangling single strand. We could repair the DNA and, while we're at it, add something else onto it. Suppose that there existed a strand of DNA for the area of skin above your upper lip and a restricted enzyme able to identify it. Then, engineers could snip it and add on a little piece, giving you a thick mustache or even a beauty mark.

○ The second opportunity is to take from. Our DNA sets in motion processes that help us maintain robust health. Part of one segment of our DNA helps produce insulin. With the appropriate restricted enzyme, engineers could split the DNA and grab the valuable insulin-producing part. They could then grow insulin in bacteria in the lab and use that insulin to save lives.

- Suppose that you want to close down your shoveling firm and moving into the burgeoning field of biomedical engineering, of which gene splicing is just one of the many techniques that your firm will use. After surveying the set of medical challenges and needs, your firm will be attempting to genetically engineer knuckles. As before, your firm will employ 12 people.

- Suppose that you post an advertisement and get hundreds of applicants. Some have doctorates in mechanical engineering, biology, medical imaging, orthopedic engineering, and tissue engineering. You could come up with some proxy for "ability" as follows: ability = years in school + quality of training + number of academic publications + strength of letters of recommendation. Assume that you have some way to measure these attributes objectively. You could then compute scores for each of the applicants.

- Alternatively, you could have all applicants take a common test. You could then hire the people who scored the highest. This would be analogous to having hole diggers dig holes for an hour and see who could dig the most.

- Either way, once you have a ranking, you could choose the best 12—but this is not a good plan. It could be that 10 of your best 12 applicants, as rated by score, work in medical imaging. You would need someone to do imaging, but you wouldn't need 10 people to do imaging. Growing knuckles requires people with diverse skills, so you cannot mindlessly just hire the best.

- You would do far better by recognizing what talents you need and making sure that you had coverage for the relevant skills. In this alternative approach, you would create classifications, including imagist, tissue engineer, mechanical engineer, bio instruments, and even biomechatronics.

- Within each of the fields, you might then decide how many people you need and hire the best. For the same reason as before, this would not be optimal. For example, the 2 best tissue engineers could lack diversity; they could have gone to the same undergraduate and graduate institutions and worked in the same lab.

- You would do far better to think of your tissue engineers in terms of their skills—specifically, in terms of their perspectives and heuristics. You should look in detail at what projects they have completed and what they are likely to bring.

- You also made a second mistake, called the silo error. By creating categories, you constructed silos based on disciplinary training. It could be that there's someone out there who doesn't fit within these silos, and it could be someone who started out in tissue engineering but then became interested in imaging. This person might not rank highly when considered as either a pure tissue engineer or a pure imagist, but his or her ability to stand between the silos and hold them together may make him or her of tremendous value to your firm.

- The lesson is that you have to evaluate the applicants in full and choose a good collection.

- Suppose that you hired your team of diverse people. Then, you'll most likely experience a diversity bonus. You'll observe one person getting stuck on a problem and another person helping him or her. You might also restructure your team based on which combinations of talents and individuals produce the most synergies.

- Hole digging is a low-dimensional problem, and if it's not difficult, then you don't need diversity—you don't need perspectives and heuristics. You just need someone to solve it or, in this case, dig it.

- However, to build a knuckle, you need knowledge of genes, restricted enzymes, tissues, imaging, and biomechanics. The various functions of a knuckle and how to reproduce them can be seen through multiple lenses, or perspectives. Similarly, there exist many techniques, or heuristics, for building the knuckle parts—and those parts interact, producing a rugged landscape.

- The process of building knuckles satisfies the 4 conditions for choosing diversity over ability. It is a difficult problem. In addition, everyone is smart relative to the problem because you can cull your applicant pool down to those who have relevant skills. Furthermore, you are choosing from a diverse pool. Finally, the group is of moderate size.

- The theory also helps you understand why you don't need diverse hole diggers, and it explains the trend toward a new thinking about the value of diversity. We're increasingly confronting problems in which diversity will help us.

Hiring and Admitting

- When you think about whom to hire, you want to consider the tools that people have. You want those people to have germane tools, but you have to be careful when you think about what those germane tools are.

- You also want to think about the ratio of hole digging to collective problem solving. The more hole digging, the more you want people who prove capable at completing individual tasks, and the more you should care about things like grade point averages and test scores. These reflect individual ability with reasonable correlation.

- On the other hand, if the job requires lots of group problem solving, you want diverse thinkers. To test for this, you could ask open-ended questions and see how someone answers. You ask these questions not to see if someone has the right answer, but to see if the applicant knows Fermi's method, reasoning by analogy, or linear decomposition. If an applicant uses different categories than other people, you might want to hire him or her.

- For more technical jobs, you might give the person a problem and see how he or she solves it. If the person solves the problem using a different method than the others, then it might be good to include that person in the mix because he or she is bringing diverse tools.

- We can apply this same sort of thinking to college admissions. Unfortunately, people often rely on hole-digging logic, resulting in frustration and missed opportunity.

- Grades don't capture wisdom. A focus on grades can lead to a less meaningful college experience as well as less postcollege success. In addition, if you focus on grades, you're going to take classes that you're going to do well in. You're not going to push yourself into interesting new areas—if you're worried about not getting a high grade. The students who do best in college are the ones who have a goal and who then choose courses so that they can accumulate tools, knowledge, and experiences that best help them achieve that goal.

Suggested Reading

Florida, *The Rise of the Creative Class*.

Questions to Consider

1. Describe a job that is mostly hole digging.

2. Why is measuring ability more difficult in the modern economy than it was 100 years ago?

Ability and Diversity
Lecture 14

Many people believe that an increase in diversity implies a reduction in ability, but there is not necessarily a tradeoff between the 2. In fact, the main point of this lecture is that we should seek to create groups and teams of diverse and able people. In addition, for a team to perform well as a group, it will be beneficial if members bring diverse sets of tools and if they share, listen, and treat one another with respect. Building the best team does not necessarily involve hiring the people who score highest on an exam.

Linear Orderings

- To further understand the relationship between ability and diversity, we first need to tackle the difference between ability and intelligence. If we say that someone is intelligent, we might mean that they have a high IQ.

- IQ tests assign a numerical score to individuals. There exist many types of intelligence tests. Some test crystallized intelligence, which is what you know. Others test fluid intelligence, which is what you're able to learn on the fly.

- Psychometricians—the people who measure intelligence—believe that something like general intelligence exists because there exists substantial correlation on these tests. If you do well on one test, you'll likely do well on another. Scores won't be perfectly correlated, but the correlations can be pretty strong.

- The people who do well with spatial reasoning tend to do well with verbal reasoning and tend to perform well on mathematical tests as well. Empirically, there does appear to exist something like general intelligence.

- Correlation across a handful of tests does not imply that there exists an ordering of people by intelligence. Unfortunately, human language—including labels such as "best" and "worst"—enables rankings, and the creation of grade point averages, SAT and ACT scores, and IQ tests reinforce those orderings by individuals by intelligence with the imprimatur of science.

- Psychometricians don't believe that we can summarize something as complex, fluid, high dimensional, and sophisticated as human intelligence with a single number. When they claim that IQ measures intelligence, they're saying that there exists some general factor—a general intelligence—that applies across a variety of domains.

- If Bobby has a higher IQ than Camilla, then we would expect him to do better on a randomly selected cognitive test. IQ would be a good predictor. However, he may not do better. The test might better fit her set of tools, and she might do better. What psychometricians call general intelligence is a factor that pops out of empirical analysis.

- Suppose that each of 100 students take 20 intelligence tests, which each have 40 questions. Every student received a plus 5 on each question that he or she gets correct and a minus 5 on each question that he or she gets incorrect. Furthermore, assume that the average score on each test equals 100, which means that students get 30 questions correct and 10 questions wrong on average.

- One way to measure the intelligence of each person would be to take his or her average score on each exam. If Alicia scores an average of 120, then her IQ would be higher than Beatriz's, who scores an average of 100.

- Charles Spearman, an inventor of intelligence tests, developed factor analysis, which allows us to measure intelligence even more accurately. Factor analysis not only takes into account a person's score, but it also takes into account the relationship between the tests and the intelligence that we're trying to measure.

- Suppose that you have coded the scores for 18 tests and that you have 2 to go. Following are the scores on those final 2 tests.

	Test 1	Test 2
Alicia	140	100
Beatriz	90	110

- Note that both students have the same averages on these 2 tests as they had overall. However, suppose that when you look at test 1 for all of the students, you see that scores correlate very strongly with their scores on the other tests. This would mean that you might want to put more weight on test 1 because it's a good test.

- Suppose that test 2 doesn't correlate at all with the scores on the other test. In fact, suppose that it isn't test data; instead, it's from a column in which students were asked their weight. Suppose that Alicia weighs 100 pounds and Beatriz weighs 110. That means that we shouldn't give that test much weight at all.

- Factor analysis determines how much weight each test should get. The weight of each test is called its factor loading. A person's IQ is therefore not his or her average score on an IQ test, but is instead a weighting of those scores using the factor loadings.

- Let's take this same idea of factor loadings and apply it not to tests themselves but to questions that go on an IQ test. Suppose that you have IQ measures for a population of people and that you want to see if some question is a good IQ test question. Suppose that 20% of the people in your population get the question correct. You want to consider 2 cases.
  - The 20% who get the question correct all come from the top 25% in IQ.
  - The 20% who get the question correct have about average IQ.

- People who construct IQ tests would find the first question really useful because it identifies high-IQ people. It captures intelligence. They would discard the second question.

- However, the second question could have been identifying some other type of intelligence, and that's one criticism of IQ tests: They're self-referential. That critique would be damning—and no one would take IQ seriously—were it not also true that if you were to send me a question and we were to find that 20% of people get it correct, we'd be much more likely to be in the first case, where the high-IQ people get it correct, than in the second case, where the people are random. In other words, something like general intelligence does seem to exist.

People who have brains that are quicker and recall information faster tend to score better on general intelligence tests.

- In addition to the 1-dimensional factor of general intelligence, factor analysis can be used to find multiple dimensions, such as quantitative and verbal intelligence or perceptual intelligence. As we add dimensions, each test can then be evaluated for how it loads on each factor.

Amending the Toolbox Model

- Suppose there exist 52 tools that someone could learn. These tools could be perspectives or heuristics—or they could represent entire fields of tools, such as unidimensional calculus or even factor analysis.

- Assume that when someone takes an IQ test, in order to get a question correct, they need to have an appropriate tool (a form of knowledge, or crystallized intelligence), and they have to apply it correctly (fluid intelligence).

- Assume that Alicia knows 15 tools and Beatriz knows 12. The only way that we can say for sure that Alicia is smarter than Beatriz would be if Alicia knows every tool that Beatriz knows. We can compute the probability of that in 3 steps. First, we can compute the number of ways that Alicia can pick her 15 tools. Then, we can compute the number of those toolboxes that contain Beatriz's 12 tools. Finally, we can divide the second number by the first to give us the probability that Alicia knows every tool that Beatriz does.

- If you do the math, there's a 1 in 450 million chance that Alicia has all of Beatriz's tools. Therefore, there's almost no way that Alicia knows every tool that Beatriz does. This deck of cards model helps us to hold 2 somewhat contradictory ideas in our heads: There is something like general intelligence—Alicia has more tools and will score better on tests—but it's not possible to say that Alicia is better than Beatriz. Almost certainly, Beatriz brings things to the table that Alicia does not.

- Let's amend the toolbox model to account for the fact that in order to learn some tools, a person needs to learn some other tools first. We can do that by placing tools on a ladder. Now, instead of there being 52 cards in a deck, and assuming that a person picks some random set of tools, we will instead place the tools on rungs of a ladder. To learn tool number 9, a person first must learn tools 1 through 8.

- In the field of mathematics, we first learn to add and then to multiply. You cannot multiply without knowing how to add. Then, you learn geometry, algebra, trigonometry, calculus, differential equations, real analysis, and so on—up the ladder.

- Alicia knows the first 15 rungs of the ladder, and Beatriz knows the first 12. Instead of there being only a 1-in-450-million chance that Alicia knows every tool that Beatriz knows, there's now a 1-in-1 chance. It is obvious that Alicia is smarter. However, this model doesn't seem quite right either.

- In thinking about mathematics, the ladder model makes sense at the beginning, but as we move up the ladder, it branches. When a person hits the calculus level, he or she might branch off and learn probability, group theory, logic, or even topology. In other words, it's not one big ladder; it's more like a tree.

- We could make a tree for every subject—a chemistry tree, a physics tree, a biology tree, and a computer science tree. There's even a cooking tree, a drawing tree, and a piano-playing tree. Metaphorically, we can think of a whole bunch of trees of various heights and various branches. Some of those trees, such as the mathematics tree, might appear to be more like a bunch of ladders emanating from a few main boughs.

- In that case in which we assumed that there was only 1 ladder, Alicia, who knows more tools, knows everything that Beatriz knows. If we add a ladder so that there are now 2 ladders, Beatriz might go 6 rungs up on each. Alicia, who can go up a total of 15 rungs, might go 0 on one and 15 on the other. She might do 1 and 14 or 2 and 12, for example, for a total of 16 possibilities. Only 4 possibilities—(6, 9), (7, 8), (8, 7), (9, 6)—contain the tools that Beatriz has, and that's true regardless of how Beatriz allocates her tools on the ladder.

- Thus, with one ladder, Alicia knows everything that Beatriz knows. With 2 ladders, that probability falls to 25%. With 3 ladders, the odds fall to less than 8%, and with 4 ladders, the percentage will be less than 2.5%.

- Each of us is a tree of knowledge and tools, and each of us is different. The toolbox/tree model offers a useful, productive way to think about capabilities and to see the relationship between ability and diversity. Ability is the number of tools that a person possesses, and it can also be thought of as the size of the tree—how may splits and how many branches the tree contains. However, people of the same ability can have very different structure to their knowledge.

Suggested Reading

Gould, *The Mismeasure of Man*.

Lemann, *The Big Test*.

Page, *The Difference*, chap. 5.

Questions to Consider

1. Why is it surprising that IQ tests work—that there is something called "general intelligence"?

2. Why do professions with more ladders make rankings by ability more difficult?

Combining and Recombining Heuristics
Lecture 15

In this lecture, you're going to learn how tools and ideas combine to create even more ideas. You will witness the awesome power of recombination from a theoretical standpoint, and you will discover that a great deal of innovation and growth in practice stems from taking existing ideas, technologies, and tools, and recombining them. Through recombination, we can make something new out of old parts, and if someone comes up with something entirely new—such as the laser, the telegraph, or superconducting materials—we can combine that new thing with existing things to create even more new things.

The Mathematics of Recombination

- The mathematics of recombination relies on 3 formulas. The first is multiplication: a times b. If you have a shirts and b pairs of pants, you can make a times b outfits. Therefore, if you have 10 pairs of pants and 15 shirts, you can make 150 outfits—setting aside the fact that some pants and shirts will not coordinate well together. In addition, if you buy 2 new pairs of paints, you get not 2 but 30 new potential outfits.

- The second formula is called n choose k, and it tells us how many ways to pick k items from a group of n. Suppose that you are trying to decide what items to put on a pizza. In your fridge, you have 12 possible toppings: 3 kinds of meat (pepperoni, sausage, and ham) and 9 types of vegetables.

- You want your pizza to have exactly 3 toppings, so how many different pizzas can you make? To answer that question, you have to find out how many possible combinations of 3 topics you can choose from 12. Mathematicians call this amount 12 choose 3.

- You have 12 things you could pick first, 11 you could pick second, and 10 you could pick third. Therefore, the answer is $12 \times 11 \times 10$. However, if you choose pepperoni, then black olives, then onion, that's the same thing as picking black olives, then onion, then pepperoni or picking onion, pepperoni, and then black olives.

- To account for all of these orders, you have to divide by the various ways you could rearrange your 3 toppings. There are 3 things that you can pick first, 2 things that you can pick second, and one thing that you can pick third, so that's just $3 \times 2 \times 1$.

- Therefore, the number of ways to pick 3 from 9 equals $(12 \times 11 \times 10) \div (3 \times 2 \times 1)$, so that's a total of 220 combinations.

- For the third formula, suppose that you want to figure out the total number of pizzas you could create if you don't restrict yourself to 3 items. To make that calculation, think of each item as being either on the pizza or off the pizza. Because you have 12 items, you can think of this as a string of 12 light switches—each one of which is either off or on.

- How many combinations are there? Well, each switch can be off or on, so that's 2 possibilities for each switch. If you had 2 switches, you would have 2 possibilities for the first and 2 possibilities for the second, so that's 2×2, or 4 possibilities. If you had 3 switches, it would be $2 \times 2 \times 2$, or 8 possibilities.

- Let's now see how these 3 formulas apply to recombination.
    - If we're combining 2 piles, the number of combinations is just the product of the number in each pile.
    - If we're picking a fixed number from a set, we use the n choose k formula, and that number grows large rapidly.
    - Finally, if we're looking at all possible combinations of attributes, we get 2 raised to the power of the number of attributes, and this can be a huge number.

- The key insight that we can draw from these 3 formulas is that the number of combinations grows as we have more and more parts.

Economic Innovation
- Ideas can be used by anyone. Economists call ideas nonrival, which means that multiple people can use them at the same time. Think of ideas as Lego blocks. As we develop more ideas, we have even more Legos to recombine to create new and exciting products, ideas, and policies. Once we have one idea, then we have even more ideas.

- Economic growth, our continued progress, rests to a substantial extent on recombination. Economic historian Joel Mokyr argues that we can explain the great increases in economic growth as occurring because we could recombine nonrival ideas.

- The idea that economic growth and innovation stem from recombination receives a more mathematical treatment in an article by Martin Weitzman called "Recombinant Growth." The core idea in the paper is simply that people develop ideas, and those ideas can be recombined.

- There are 5 observations relevant to the theory of recombination that will enable us to see when and how recombinations occur in practice.

Observation 1: There can be too much of a good thing.
- Weitzman's model demonstrates an overabundance of possibility due to recombination. As we know from the math we did at the beginning of the lecture, there will be just too many ideas to pursue. Whether we're taking one idea from one pile and one idea from another pile or whether we're choosing a set of options, we have an abundance of options. The challenge, therefore, is not to generate ideas—but to pick from among them.

Observation 2: Not all combinations can be combined.

- Throughout, we've assumed that any 2 ideas can be combined, but that's not always true. Many times, there isn't as much of an overabundance as you might think. Perhaps most of the ideas that people have don't make any sense, but a nonsensical idea might open up the category of ideas that leads to a winning idea.

Observation 3: Not all useful combinations get tried.

- Another reason that we may not have the abundance that recombination would produce is that we're often blind to ideas. We only see narrow opportunities. Evolution has an advantage over creative human systems in that it tries all mutations. People often get stuck in cognitive ruts and don't think of all the possibilities.

Observation 4: One big reason that we don't try all combinations is that the ideas don't get to meet one another.

- Ideas are in our heads and then eventually in books and articles, but each of us can have only so many ideas in our heads, and we can only combine the ideas that exist within our heads. Alternatively, we can combine our ideas with those of people with whom we interact, but people tend to interact with people who are like them. Instead of having all of the ideas in one big soup and all possible combinations boiling up, we have ideas bumping into one another only when people who have those ideas bump into one another.

- This insight allows us to understand why some product classes exhibit lots of growth and others do not. Essentially, you can think of innovation as involving either small-step improvements made by specialists or by breakthroughs—called creeps and leaps, respectively. The leaps have 2 sources: recombination and new perspectives. The creeps come about by people applying new, and therefore diverse, heuristics to a problem. Heuristics make small movements up the hill; recombination and new perspectives take giant leaps.

- Who should we have interacting with one another? If we have lots of specialists, then we'll have a lot of heuristics, so we should be able to do lots of local climbing, but we shouldn't make big leaps. Therefore, in the short term, this is good, but it is not so good for long-term growth.

- On the other hand, we might have lots of people looking to combine ideas—who are sometimes referred to as knowledge brokers because they broker ideas between areas. If we think of **networks** of ideas, the knowledge brokers fill holes in the network of ideas by connecting disparate knowledge bases.

- Suppose that you have a firm that makes stoves. Your firm consists primarily of engineers, who work on the production side, and marketing and design people, who try to figure out what people want. You could imagine an organizational structure that contains 2 clusters: a cluster of marketing people and a cluster of engineers. These 2 clusters might then be connected by a third, smaller cluster called management.

- If you have all knowledge brokers, then you get lots of big ideas, but they don't get refined. Therefore, if you want to ask how you drive growth in an area such as Silicon Valley, most economists and strategy professionals would say that you need lots of specialists—because the area is loaded with doctorates in computer science and math—and you need lots of knowledge brokers because the area might have the largest concentration of venture capitalists in the world. The 2 together produce tremendous growth.

- If you hire a whole bunch of specialists and put them in isolation, they'll be good at doing the specific task they were assigned—such as building the atomic bomb at Los Alamos, one of the great successes in the history of sequestration of talent—but they're not going to produce novel recombinant ideas.

Observation 5: To create incentives to produce ideas, we let people own them—at least for a while.

- Ideas and technological breakthroughs produce 3 benefits: direct benefits, combinatoric benefits, and perspective benefits, which can change how we see the world.

- The value of ideas implies that we should create incentives for people to create them. In other words, we should let people own their ideas. That's why governments create patents. If you come up with a new idea, you can patent it and people then have to pay you to use the idea. In this way, people who make ideas make money.

- In recent years, people have come to question whether that way of thinking makes sense. These scholars argue that the people who developed the ideas benefit from first-mover advantage. They also argue that patent costs can be so prohibitive that they preclude exploration of the recombinations of ideas that could drive growth. Fortunately, people cannot patent the perspectives that come about from a new idea, and those perspectives can spread far and wide.

- Recombination contributes to economic growth. In fact, many of the big improvements to our standard of living—such as putting wheels on steam engines to make trains, putting engines in horseless carriages, and even putting books on the Internet—have come about by recombining ideas that already existed.

Important Term

network: A collection of nodes and links, or connections between the nodes.

Suggested Reading

Page, *Diversity and Complexity*, chap. 3.

Weitzman, "Recombinant Growth."

1. What are the 3 formulas for recombination?

2. What are the 5 observations that are relevant to the theory of recombination that enable us to see when and how recombinations occur in practice?

Beware of False Prophets—No Free Lunch
Lecture 16

In this lecture, you're going to learn about the ubiquity and contingency of heuristics. You will see that often a heuristic from one domain can apply in other domains. Perhaps most importantly, you will learn that heuristics are conditional. Across all problems, no heuristic will perform any better than any other. In other words, there's no free lunch. That doesn't mean that there won't be good heuristics for particular classes of problems—because there will—but it does mean that if you face a really hard problem, you want to have lots of heuristics available.

Formal versus Informal Heuristics

- There are 2 types of heuristics: formal heuristics, which are mathematical and algorithmic, and informal heuristics.

- Some of the first heuristics we learn relate to multiplication. Suppose that we want to multiply 2 numbers—for example, 16 and 18. We could multiply the entire product the way that we were taught to do in elementary school. First, we multiply 8 by 6 to get 48. Next, we multiply 8 by 10 to get 80. Then, we multiply 10 by 6 to get 60 and 10 by 10 to get 100. Finally, we add all 4 numbers: $48 + 80 + 60 + 100 = 288$.

- However, we can come up with a few heuristics that we might use to solve this problem more quickly. Our first heuristic relies on squares: 16 times 18 is just 16 times 16—a square—with 2 times 16 left over. This heuristic works well if you know your squares. If you do, you know that $16^2 = 256$. Then, $16 \times 2 = 32$, and $256 + 32 = 288$.

- There's an even better heuristic that is based on algebra. Notice that 16 times 18 equals 17 minus 1 times 17 plus 1. Take any number x. If we multiply $(x - 1)(x + 1)$, we get $x^2 - x + x - 1$, or $x^2 - 1$. Therefore, $16 \times 18 = 17^2 - 1$, which is $289 - 1$, or 288.

- All 3 of these heuristics are formal heuristics. They are algorithms—rules that we can follow to arrive at an answer or a new solution.

- Formal heuristics can be much more complicated than these 3. We can, for example, think of linear regression as a heuristic. In this case, it's a heuristic for identifying patterns in data and relationships between variables. Though regression won't verify whether a relationship is causal, it can tell us the magnitude of a relationship and its significance, or the likelihood that we have the right direction for the relationship.

- For example, suppose that you want to determine whether people take into account fuel efficiency when purchasing a car. The regression model heuristic involves gathering data on car sales, running a regression, and then seeing if people are more likely to buy cars that get better mileage or if cars that get better mileage sell for a premium. This approach won't definitely give you the answer because the data could be misleading or correlated in some strange way, but it will be informative.

- Regression is a formal heuristic, which means that it has a mathematical representation and formula that is used to come up with an answer. It's not something that you can do in your head—at least not easily.

- Informal heuristics, on the other hand, we can do in our heads. The rules we use to get around in the world are informal heuristics. Gerd Gigerenzer, a German academic, wrote a widely read book called *Simple Heuristics That Make Us Smart*. In this book, Gigerenzer argues that people accumulate collections of heuristics over their lives. We abandon those that seem not to work, and we sort of figure out which will work where, and eventually, armed with some simple rules, we do pretty well.

- The accuracy of a heuristic need not be correlated in any way with its sophistication. We need only to think of housing or stock-market bubbles that have collapsed. In each case, people have made sophisticated arguments about why the bubble isn't really a bubble. However, in each case, a simple heuristic—that markets cannot consistently go up by x% per year unless the economy is growing by x% per year (what some call long-term market efficiency)—performs well.

- Referring to the rugged landscape model, at any point in time, each of us will be stuck on lots of local optima—in our home lives, work lives, and social lives—and there are 2 ways to get off those local peaks to new, higher peaks. First, a new perspective rearranges all of the possibilities so that what was once a local peak may now be on the side of a hill. Second, a new heuristic lets us move about our landscape in a new direction.

- Heuristics help guide us, and we want to amass a great many of them. At the same time, we should be a little bit skeptical. It cannot be the case that these simple heuristics always work.

The Conditionality of Heuristics

- Heuristics are conditional. They work in some cases, but they don't work in others. That's why we should think of heuristics as not just rules to follow but as conditional rules. This is one big reason that scientists construct formal models and don't just tell stories. A model makes formal assumptions so that we know the conditions under which a result holds and doesn't hold.

- We can think of the proverbs "2 heads are better than 1" and "too many cooks spoil the broth" as heuristics. The first implies that we should get a diverse team together, but the second says not to do that. These seem to contradict.

- In predictive contexts, more heads are better, but on irreversible projects, diversity can create problems. Recall the story about adding chicken broth to the vegetarian soup. Cooking is irreversible.

- As for the idea that 2 heads are better than 1, there have been 2 cases so far in which that held. First, on predictive tasks, the diversity prediction theorem states that 2 equally good diverse predictions will be more accurate, on average, than either prediction alone. In addition, the diversity-trumps-ability theorem states that when solving problems, we'd rather have 2 heads than 1—provided that certain conditions are met.

- The idea of the conditionality of heuristics—the fact that they only work given certain conditions are met—leads us into what is known as the **no free lunch theorem**. This theorem, developed by David Wolpert and William Macready, states that any 2 heuristics that look at the same number of possible answers or solutions will be equally good across all problems.

- Suppose that we have a mathematical function defined over the negative and positive integers, but we don't know what that function is. It's just some function $f(x)$. However, if given a number—7, for example—we can learn the value of the function at $x = 7$.

- Suppose we're at 5, and we know that the function has a value of 14 at 5. Mathematically, we would say $f(5) = 14$.

- Let's compare 4 reasonable search heuristics. If we don't know anything about f, they're all equally good.
  - Increase x by 1.
  - Decrease x by 1.
  - Choose negative x.
  - Pick a random x.

- The no free lunch theorem tells us that if we don't know anything about the function, then we have no reason to choose any heuristic over any other—provided that those heuristics test the same number of possible solutions.

Digging Deeper: Covey and Collins

- Let's employ the logic of the no free lunch theorem to 2 advice books: Stephen Covey's *The 7 Habits of Highly Effective People* and Jim Collins's *Good to Great*.

- One of Covey's rules is "big rocks first." Suppose that you're given the task of filling a bucket. You have both big rocks and small rocks. How do you do it? Well, you should put the big rocks in first. If you put the big rocks in first and then the small ones, the small ones will fill in the gaps. If you put the small ones in first, you won't be able to fit in the big ones.

- This seems like good advice, but it has an opposite proverb: Take care of the little things, and the big things will take care of themselves. Covey is saying that he knows a lot about the business world, and even though there are an equal number of big-rocks-first problems and little-rocks-first problems that exist in theory, in practice, that's not true. If you look at those problems that you're likely to encounter in the business world, there exist far more big-rocks-first problems.

- The big-rocks-first heuristic is a good one to have in your toolbox, but be skeptical of applying it in all cases.

- Collins devoted large amounts of time and effort determining what makes a successful company, and he came up with a list of the features—some of which are heuristics—of great companies.

- In his book, Collins took a bold step. He identified 11 companies that adhered to his principles. However, the following information shows how Collins's 11 great companies fared in the decade following his book's publication. During this period, the market was flat—0%.

Company Name	Financial Standing
Abbott Laboratories	Stock up 0%
Circuit City	Bankrupt
Fannie Mae	Placed in conservatorship
Gillette	Bought by P&G
Kimberly-Clark	Stock up 1%
Kroger	Stock up 0%
Nucor	Stock up 4-fold
Philip Morris	Stock down 20%
Pitney Bowes	Stock down 20%
Walgreens	Stock up 0%
Wells Fargo	Stock up 0%

- Obviously, these companies did not do very well. However, Collins was not necessarily wrong. What he found were heuristics that worked well from 1990–2000. The same ones did not work as well in the following 10 years.

- As the world changes, we can think of the rugged landscape as dancing—called a **dancing landscape**—which implies that what worked then may not work now. It may also imply that what didn't work then may be the idea that we need at the moment. That's why it's good to accumulate heuristics and to recognize their conditionality.

Important Terms

dancing landscape: A fitness or payoff landscape that is coupled so that when one entity changes its action, it causes the other entity's landscape to shift.

no free lunch theorem: Any 2 heuristics that test the same number of points have the same expected value across all possible problems.

Page, *The Difference*, chap. 2.

Wolpert and Macready, "No Free Lunch Theorems for Optimization."

Questions to Consider

1. Why does the no free lunch theorem say that we shouldn't always put big rocks in first?

2. What are 3 heuristics that mathematicians use?

Crowdsourcing and the Limits of Diversity
Lecture 17

In this lecture, you're going to learn about crowdsourcing, which involves tapping into the power of information technology to get large numbers of diverse people working on a problem. The story of the Netflix Prize competition will be mashed up with 2 core lessons about diversity and problem solving to help you understand how crowdsourcing really works. You'll also apply what you've learned about crowdsourcing to 2 broader questions: How big should a group be? How much diversity should it have?

Leveraging Diversity

- One thing that we can conclude from what we have learned so far is that we should have lots of diverse people working on problems. That logic underpins the success of pluralistic market economies.

- A free market allows everyone to contribute; no one is politically excluded. This means that, in theory, anyone can work on any problem. The fact that problems have market values associated with them also means that more people should tend to work on problems that produce more economic rents.

- Clearly, however, some caveats are in order. For example, markets create distortions in the way that more energy is spent thinking about how to satisfy the desires of rich people than those of poor people, but it's not inaccurate to say that market incentives bias effort toward more important problems.

- A vast majority of that problem solving occurs in secret. It's done by private firms that don't have any incentives to share it, and it's done by government agencies who want to keep what they learn private. Some research and development is done in universities, and most of that is out in the open, but that's only a part of all research and development—probably 10%.

- The problem is that companies such as Microsoft and Pfizer spend billions of dollars on research and development but don't necessarily share what they learn because they're trying to take what they learn and turn it into better product and, hopefully, larger market share and profits.

- One cost of not sharing is that it means that fewer people can provide input into their problems. This means that they're not getting the best solutions they could get—or the best product they could get. Firms are learning to open up a bit—for example, the Netflix Prize competition—and to allow lots of people to work on their problems through **crowdsourcing**, which is a term that was coined by Jeff Howe.

- Crowdsourcing opens up a problem to a population or community often with a minimum of coordination. Crowdsourcing leverages the capabilities of populations that have diverse ways of finding solutions, and it has proven to be successful in writing open-source code, producing consumer goods and medical devices, and designing vehicles and buildings. Unpacking those successes reveals a mixture of causes. Crowdsourced competitions attract problem solvers with diverse perspective and heuristics, which is why this method works.

- The Netflix Prize competition is a famous example of a crowdsourced competition. Another famous example involves looking for gold. A Canadian mining company called Goldcorp has a mine in Ontario, and it wasn't producing as much gold as they thought it should, so they had a competition in which people could help them find the gold. Goldcorp posted all of the information they had about the mine on the Internet, and they gave prizes to people or teams who identified the most gold.

- A diverse group of smart people participated and identified over 100 places to look for gold—and over 1/2 of these places were new. When the contest began, the mine was producing 53,000 ounces per year, and after the contest, it was producing 504,000 ounces per year. The cost of getting that gold fell from $369 per ounce to $59 per ounce. The value of the mine also made a jump from around $100 million to $9 billion, which is 90 times the value.

- One of the first people to systematically leverage diversity through crowdsourcing was Alph Bingham, who set up a company called InnoCentive. The business model of InnoCentive involves businesses posting a problem on the InnoCentive website along with a reward for a solution. Originally, InnoCentive mostly concentrated on problems in the pharmaceutical realm, but now they've branched out.

- Suppose, for example, you want to find a harmless chemical solution that will turn blue whenever it comes into contact with ammonia. Well, you just post it on the InnoCentive website, and they send it out to their problem-solving community. That community has over 100,000 people in it, and they are all searching for problems that they might be able to solve.

- InnoCentive solves around 40% of the problems that get posted. This is incredible—given that these were problems that couldn't be solved. How can it be that a company like Pfizer that spends billions on research cannot solve a problem, but InnoCentive can?

- The answer is diversity. InnoCentive taps into a broader collection of scientists. Research has shown that problems that are posed with greater generality attract a more diverse set of problem solvers and are more likely to be solved.

- The challenges that are posted on the InnoCentive website are not posed as mathematics, physics, chemistry, or materials science problems. They are just posed as problems. As a result, they should attract a diverse set of problem solvers who want to earn money for their contributions. Open-ended questions more often attract the marginal problem solvers, who are likely to find solutions.

- Crowdsourcing can consist of having groups of people collectively working on a task, decomposing a big problem into smaller problems, or an open competition.

Limitations of Crowdsourcing
- There are 3 problems with crowdsourcing: the problem of sharing, genius or gadget, and pay to play.

The Problem of Sharing
- Most research is done in firms that don't always want to share what they know. For their competition, Netflix released a lot of data about movie rentals and people, but that information could not be used by anyone else because users' names were kept private. Even if someone else did use the information, Netflix didn't see how some competitor could use it to cut into Netflix's market share.

- Goldcorp posted a ton of information about their mine, but they own the mine, and that information is only of value to the person who owns the mine. Thus, the costs of putting that information on the Internet were low.

- With InnoCentive, problems are posted anonymously and out of context. Procter and Gamble may be able to post a problem that, if solved, would enable them to create a chemical process that would create a shampoo that straightens curly hair without any competitors knowing what they're up to.

Genius or Gadget

- The most vocal critics of crowdsourcing don't point to the sharing problem even though they acknowledge it. Instead, they argue that crowds won't produce anything of genius. Mozart wasn't a crowd, and neither was Einstein.

- However, science has become team based. Teams drove the innovations at Bell Laboratories, and they drive innovations at companies such as Apple, Google, Microsoft, and Genentech.

- The argument that crowds cannot produce the sublime has merit. It gets its most coherent voice in an engaging book by Jaron Lanier titled *You Are Not a Gadget: A Manifesto*. Lanier, a muse of the tech community, makes 2 points that are relevant to this course.
  - He argues that everyone commenting on everything has led to lots of so-called raw opinion being voiced. The result is that we often end up with banal groupthink, locking us into inefficient platforms and paradigms.
  - He also argues that nothing transcendent or beautiful will come from lots of people kibitzing on problems.

- Transcendent ideas tend to come from individuals, but those individuals tend to be in diverse, vibrant communities. Moreover, even transcendence gets refined. For example, even poets have editors. In more pragmatic pursuits, kibitzing appears to add substantial value.

- On a conjunctive task, everything is related to and connected to everything else. Writing a novel or an opera is conjunctive. In contrast, disjunctive tasks can be separated, and the parts can be solved in isolation.

- The Netflix Prize, the Goldcorp challenge, and the types of problems that InnoCentive posts aren't conjunctive tasks. That is why we can open them up to crowds. That's not to say that we're not getting better at having teams and larger groups—even crowds—take on conjunctive tasks.

- It's only partially true that great books are not written by teams. Read the acknowledgements page of any book and notice all of the people that the author thanks for helping with the research and the writing.

- Think of crowdsourcing as a heuristic—a way to solve problems. Heuristics are contingent. Just like the big-rocks-first heuristic, crowdsourcing won't work on all problems, but it will work on some. The goal is to figure out which problems it will work on.

Pay to Play
- The final concern regarding crowdsourcing turns on costs and benefits. Given the negligible monetary incentives of most crowdsourcing examples, crowdsourced design must rely on other motivations. People must implicitly pay to play.

- The incentives to contribute need not be monetary. They can include the novelty of participating, the opportunity to build human capital, the comparison of one's skills and techniques against competitors, a deep concern or stake in the ultimate design (this holds for crowdsourced prosthetic design), or the building of one's reputation.

When to Crowdsource and How Much Diversity Is Optimal
- Crowdsourcing, by definition, takes up the time and effort of many people, regardless of whether those people are paid. Therefore, you should only crowdsource—or, for that matter, assign a problem to a team—if it's important. The harder and more important the problem, the more you need to figure out how to tap into diversity.

- We know that the more people and the more diverse those people think, the more perspectives we'll have, and the more heuristics we'll have applied to our problem. This means that we'll have more ideas on the table. Decades of research in problem solving demonstrates that given a problem, diverse, larger groups generate more solutions than small, homogeneous groups.

- By tossing a design problem out to an enormous diverse group, crowdsourcing produces loads of solutions—but that may not be good. Abundant research also shows that many of these ideas will be incoherent or of low value. In addition, when confronted with thousands of possibilities, groups become cognitively overloaded and can often make bad choices.

- If you have a million solutions, you need some way to accurately, quickly, and cheaply evaluate them. This is called an oracle. Crowdsourced problem solving works best when there's an oracle. The Netflix Prize had an almost perfect oracle: People could test their models against samples of the data set.

- Problems without oracles are harder to crowdsource. Something doesn't have to be complex to lack an oracle; it could be low dimensional and not complex.

- The future lies in using diverse crowds as oracles—in other words, using diversity twice. First, you use the power of diverse perspectives and solutions to come up with solutions. Then, you use the power of diverse predictive models to decide which is best.

Important Term

crowdsourcing: Using large numbers of people to find a solution to a problem—usually done over the Internet.

Suggested Reading

Howe, *Why the Power of the Crowd Is Driving the Future of Business*.

Questions to Consider

1. Why do oracles improve one's ability to crowdsource a problem?

2. What is meant by double crowdsourcing?

Experimentation, Variation, and Six Sigma
Lecture 18

O ver the past few lectures, you have been learning about the role of diversity in prediction and problem solving. In the next few lectures, you're going to learn about the relationship between diversity and robustness, which is the ability of a system to maintain functionality—to keep doing what it's doing. When designing or engineering systems—whether the systems are human, mechanical, or electronic—people strive for both efficiency (getting good outcomes) and robustness (maintaining those outcomes in the face of external shocks and internal dynamics). This lecture will focus on the roles that variation plays on robustness.

Diversity versus Variation

- There isn't a stark contrast between diversity and variation. Diversity means differences in types. A diverse ecosystem, such as an African savannah, supports many different types of animals—including wildebeests, zebras, lions, giraffes, and elephants. Variation means differences within a type, such as the variation in the size and color within the population of African elephants.

- Variation can refer to the subtle differences in how people perform a task. Variation can be seen as error or as exploration. If it is seen as error, we want to reduce it. If you're making medical instruments, for example, you don't want variation—you want precision. However, suppose that you're in a very fluid, competitive environment, such as politics, software, or an ecosystem. In these cases, variation may be seen as exploration and may be desired.

- Scientists describe variation with distributions, which give the probabilities of various values. If you're looking at the heights of adult male giraffes on a graph, they might be distributed in a familiar bell curve, in which case the mean (or the average) lies at the center of the bell curve. Because the bell curve is symmetric, the mean is also equal to the median.

- The bell curve, or normal distribution, appears frequently. The heights and weights of any species—including humans—and the number of points scored by a basketball team will be normally distributed.

Height of Adult Male Giraffes

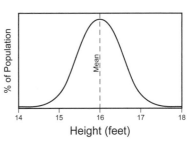

- For a variety of processes, particularly those in which a lot of different parts add up to create the whole, variation will be normally distributed. For example, a man's height is the sum of the lengths of his lower legs and upper legs plus the length of his torso, neck, and head. The head, in turn, can be further broken down into parts. Even if each of these variables isn't normally distributed, the sum will be, provided that there are enough variables and that they have finite variance. This is called the central limit theorem.

- We can characterize a normal distribution with just 2 parameters: mean and standard deviation. The mean is the average value. Because the bell curve is symmetric, it's also the median, or the value in the middle. The standard deviation tells us the spread, or how much.

- The fact that only 2 parameters define the distribution means that any 2 normal distributions are identical—up to relabeling the axis. The distribution of heights of men, which has a mean of about 5 feet 10 inches with a standard deviation of about 2.8 inches (approximately 3) looks exactly the same as the distribution of the weights of chickadee, which has a mean of about 11 grams and a standard deviation of about 1 gram. In both cases, if we go 1 standard deviation to the left and right of the mean, we get 68% of the values. Therefore, 68% of men are between 5 feet 7 inches and 6 feet 1 inch, and 68% of chickadees are between 10 and 12 grams.

- In addition, 95% of the values will be within 2 standard deviations, and 99% will be within 3 standard deviations. That means that 99% of all men are between 5 feet 1 inch and 6 feet 7 inches. It also means that you're not likely to see a chickadee tipping the scales at 14 grams. Statisticians denote the standard deviation by the Greek letter sigma.

- This very same sigma has become a big idea in management. The Six Sigma movement, which began at Motorola, is antivariation. In production processes, variation in output is a bad thing.

Six Sigma

- **Six Sigma** refers to 6 standard deviations, which is 99.99966% of all possible outcomes. A man who is 6 standard deviations above the mean would be about 18 inches above the mean, or 7 feet 4 inches. This means that you would expect only 3.4 men to be that tall per million.

- To understand how Six Sigma thinking works, suppose that you own a company that makes bunk beds. You design the beds so that the top and bottom bunks connect by dowels. The dowels fit into holes drilled into the top of the bottom bunk posts and holes drilled into the bottom of the top bunk legs so that the top can be pegged into the bottom.

- These dowels should be 1 inch in diameter. However, they're made on a lathe, and some will be a little bigger than an inch and some a little smaller. A distribution of the set of dowel diameters will have a mean of 1 and a standard deviation of 0.03 inches.

- If the dowel is too wide, it won't fit in the hole. Assume that the hole is drilled to be 1.06 inches in diameter. If the dowel is too narrow, the bed will wobble. Suppose that you do some consumer testing and find that if the diameter is less than 0.94 inches, the bed is too wobbly and consumers will complain but that if it's thicker than 0.94 inches, customers don't complain.

- As long as you're within 2 standard deviations, the bed will function; otherwise, it won't. This means that 95% of the time, the dowel will fit, but 5% of the time, it won't. There are 4 dowels per bed, which means that almost 20% of all beds will have a dowel that doesn't fit. That's too many; your company will fold. If you adopt Six Sigma thinking, however, then you will reduce variation so that failure only occurs if the variation is 6 standard deviations, or 6 sigmas, from the mean.

- Variation in the Six Sigma framework hurts performance, and you want to reduce it. To reduce variation, a technique that's recently gained traction is the checklist. Pilots have long used checklists because safety is a huge concern on airplanes. Recently, doctors have started using checklists as well.

Variation as Experimentation

- We don't always want to reduce variation. Variation enables us to climb those rugged peaks in our rugged landscape to find better solutions. Adopting Six Sigma thinking means that we stop trying new things, and that's only a good idea if we're at a peak.

- When trying a new recipe, most people try to adhere closely to the directions. However, the second time you try the recipe, you might introduce a little variation. By trying new variations, you're moving around a little on the rugged landscape with the hope of finding a point of even higher elevation.

- Recall that annealing is the process through which glass and crystals form. You initially heat the glass (allow lots of variation), and then you cool it (allow very little variation). The same logic holds in many settings. In the beginning, it makes sense to experiment quite a bit—to introduce a lot of variation. This will enable jumping over the jagged peaks in the rugged landscape. Eventually, though, once you think that you're near the global peak, you want to slow down, or anneal, your rate of experimentation. Eventually, you put your rate of experimentation at 0 and reenter the land of Six Sigma.

- On a fixed problem, you only need variation during the learning phase. At some point, when you're pretty sure that you're at the highest peak that you're going to find, you should reduce the amount of variation and fully adopt Six Sigma. However, the world doesn't stay fixed. In a changing world, variation becomes even more important. It allows for **adaptation**. In fact, the more variation, the faster the rate of adaptation.

Darwin's Finches

- Suppose that all of Darwin's finches had beaks of the same diameter—so there is no variation. Suppose that those beaks were the ideal size to stick into the holes in trees produced by a particular type of ant, which was the only food available to the finches.

- Suppose that a particular ant colony mutates and becomes slightly smaller so that the finches' beaks no longer fit in the ant holes. These ants will produce more new colonies than the original ants; they will take over because none are eaten. Now, the finches will die off because they can no longer eat ants.

- However, suppose that some of the finches have slightly narrow beaks. These finches could eat the new ants and would survive. Variability, therefore, allows adaptation. In fact, the more variation you have, the faster you can adapt.

- In biology, Fisher's theorem states that the rate of adaptation is proportional to the variation. Loosely speaking, if your sigma gets twice as big, then you can adapt twice as quickly. In general, the speed of adaptation correlates with variation. The more variation, the faster that a species can adapt. The logic of Fisher's theorem runs counter to that of the Six Sigma idea. According to Fisher's theorem, when the world is changing, you want variation to be able to adapt.

The Error-Adaptability Tradeoff

- In most situations, the logic of both Six Sigma and Fisher's theorem apply. If we want to exploit what works best, then we want sigma low. However, we also want to be able to explore to see if there's something better. If we reduce all variation and the environment changes, then we would likely find ourselves doing something far from optimal, but if we make sigma huge, then we're rarely doing what is best. Therefore, we want to choose a level of variation that balances the desire to not make too many errors against having the flexibility to adapt.

- In biology, the idea that evolution is smarter than people is known as Orgel's law, and it's often true. Evolution has found solutions to problems that are breathtaking in their sophistication. Evolution has also had a long time to work on the question of how to choose a level of variation.

- In nature, the level of variation depends on how species reproduce. If reproduction is asexual, then mutation is the primary driver of variation. In sexual reproduction, genetic crossover amplifies variation by taking parts of the mother and parts of the father.

- The same is true in our economic, social, and political worlds. When something works, there's a lot of selective pressure to keep it right where it is. However, when the world is about to change and when people know this, we may see lots of variation as people try to jump ahead of the curve. At moments when trends are about to change and paradigms are about to shift, variation may increase because no one really knows what to do.

Important Terms

adaption: A change in behavior or actions in response to a payoff or fitness function.

Six Sigma: Refers to the region within 6 standard deviations of the mean.

Suggested Reading

Page, *Diversity and Complexity*, chap. 5.

Pande, Neuman, and Cavanagh, *The Six Sigma Way*.

Questions to Consider

1. How does variation enhance robustness?

2. Why would the same organization promote both Six Sigma thinking and increased variation?

Diversity and Robustness
Lecture 19

I n the previous lecture, you learned how to best balance exploration and exploitation. You also observed how variation enabled systems to be more robust by making the system more likely to respond to change and able to respond faster. In this lecture, you are going to learn about the relationship between diversity and robustness—which is more complex than it might seem to be—and how possessing a diverse set of tools or investments enhances robustness. Specifically, you will learn about 3 ways in which diversity improves robustness: portfolio effects, variety, and redundancy.

Portfolio Effects

- The most widely known and understood mechanism through which diversity operates is portfolio effects. Portfolio theory originated in finance and was developed to show how diversification spreads risk. Ideally, an investor would select investments so that regardless of what happens, he or she will make money. This is accomplished by choosing a diverse set of investments. However, you cannot just pick any diverse set of investments and hope to have a portfolio that performs well—allows you to keep functioning—regardless of what happens to the stock market.

- In mathematics and finance, the concept of the state of the world refers to all of the relevant information about what's happening.

- For example, the weather possibilities for a given day include rain, hot, cold, and just right. If you're having a picnic, you could classify the weather into 4 states of the world: tent, Slip 'n Slide, fire pit, and Frisbee. Suppose that you can make some investments to make sure that the picnic succeeds. You could purchase a tent awning, a Slip 'n Slide, a fire pit, and a Frisbee. It's not the diversity of the things you bought to ensure that the picnic succeeds; instead, it's the fact that they pay off in different states of the world.

- To make a good portfolio, we need diversity relative to payoffs in the various states of the world. Financial analysts have a measure for this type of diversity called **beta**, which is a Greek letter. Suppose that you have all of your money in one asset, a house. That house will have some variation in its payoffs because in some states of the world—when the local economy is good—the value of the house will go up. In other states of the world—when the local economy is bad—the value of the house will fall.

- The **covariance** between 2 investments captures how similar their payoffs are in the various states of the world. To calculate the covariance for 2 investments (a and b), m_a denotes the average payoff in a across all states of the world, and m_b denotes the average payoff in b across all states of the world. Then, for each state of the world, take the value of a (v_a) minus the mean of a and multiply it by the value of b (v_b) minus the mean of b.

- Covariance can be 0, positive, or negative. If 2 events are unrelated, or independent, then the covariance will be 0. If they tend to move in the same direction, then they will be positively correlated. If they move in opposite directions, then they will be negatively correlated.

- Using stocks a and b as examples, negative correlation means that when a is high, b is low, and vice versa. Thus, when ($v_a - m_a$) is positive, ($v_b - m_b$) will be negative, so the covariance will be negative.

- If 2 events are independent, then the covariance tends to be neither positive nor negative; in other words, when a is above the mean, it's just as likely that b is above the mean as it is that b is below the mean.

- The beta between b and a is the ratio of the covariance of a and b to the variance of a.

- If you already have one investment (*a*) and buy *b*, if you buy a *b* that has a high beta, you have more risk. If beta is big, that means that when *a* goes up, *b* goes up. If you buy an investment with a low beta—ideally, a negative beta—then you are exposed to less risk. In fact, if you could find 2 investments that both were expected to make money with a beta of −1, this would mean that *b* would go up when *a* did worse than you expected and down when *a* did better than expected. No matter what happens, you would make money.

- When stock managers talk about creating a diverse portfolio, they mean putting together stocks that have low betas relative to one another. If you can find diverse investments (those low betas with respect to one another), then you can reduce your risk. Diversity makes people robust to changes in the economy.

- An ideal portfolio consists of investments that pay off in different states of the world, and that same logic also applies to people. Suppose that you run a consulting company or law firm. The state of the world could represent the type of problem, and the employees are investments. To be able to serve your clients, you need employees (investments) that can solve different problems (pay off in different states of the world). A pretty tight analogy can be drawn, but it's not quite satisfying because diverse problem solvers aren't really just spreading risk. They're solving different types of problems.

- To get a slightly different insight, a problem that arises can be thought of as a disturbance, and a person's tools can be thought of as being capable of responding to that disturbance or not.

Ashby's Law of Requisite Variety
- **Ashby's law of requisite variety** originated in the field of systems dynamics and applies to situations that require responses to external disturbances. Imagine waiting for some opportunity or some crisis and then having the responsibility of responding. Proactive maneuvers are not allowed. All choices are reactive to external stimuli. The law of requisite variety states that for every perturbation, there must exist an action to counter it.

- Consider the task of keeping a bathtub in working order. One thing that could go wrong with the bathtub is that the plumbing washers on the spigot could wear out. Call this event a disturbance. If a washer wears out, you then fix it. Call this a response. One day, unexpectedly, the drain springs a leak (a second disturbance). If you do nothing, you get a wet floor. If you take your one possible action—replacing the plumbing washer—then you also get a wet floor. Changing the washer won't fix the problem; instead, you have to patch the hole in the drain. The second disturbance needs a second response. The law of requisite variety states that the number of responses should equal the number of disturbances.

- The law of requisite variety provides an insight into well-functioning systems. The diversity of potential responses must be sufficient to handle the diversity of disturbances. If disturbances become more diverse, then so must the possible responses. If not, the system will not hold together. These responses must be generated, and generating potential responses is costly. Over time, the number of responses generated should tend to equal the number of disturbances because those responses that never get evoked should atrophy.

- Consider raising a child. Young children produce approximately 4 types of disturbances: hungry, wet, tired, and sick. These require 4 responses: feed, change, put in car seat and drive around town for 2 hours, and take to the doctor. As children get older, the number of disturbances grows, and the number of responses must grow accordingly. A teenager disturbed by a relationship issue won't be calmed by 1 of those 4 responses, so the law of requisite variety states that the parent must develop new responses to counteract the new types of disturbances.

- The logic that we want diverse teams because we want a portfolio can be revised to the notion that diverse teams have requisite variety, which is only one reason of many reasons for cognitive diversity. Portfolio thinking says that cognitive diversity spreads risk. Requisite-variety thinking says that diversity allows us to respond to multiple disturbances—but cognitive diversity can do a lot more.

- Organizations within the economy, which is a complex system, must satisfy something like the law of requisite variety. In the strategy literature, the tasks that an organization executes well are referred to as its core competencies, which can be thought of as responses. If these responses are well suited to the likely disturbances, then the organization should be successful. No matter what the world offers up, the firm can handle it. If, on the other hand, an organization lacks sufficient core competencies, it may be headed for disaster.

- However, that does not mean that they should be more diversified. When a firm buys another firm or enters a new industry, the firm takes on all of the disturbances of that new enterprise as well, and it needs the requisite variety of tools to handle those disturbances. As long as the new venture has a set of disturbances similar enough to those of the original firm, all is well. For every disturbance, management must have a response.

- If, however, the new disturbances differ from the acquiring firm's existing set of disturbances, the takeover may be a disaster. The acquiring firm may lack the requisite response variety. The lesson seems obvious: Do not acquire businesses that require different skill sets. Harley Davidson, for example, should not buy a grocery store chain because Harley Davidson's core competencies probably do not include responses that pertain to food spoilage.

- So far, we have only addressed one side of Ashby's law—namely, that we need to have at least as many responses as there are disturbances. Ashby's law also says that we don't need any more responses as there are disturbances. For example, the leaky drain in your bathroom does not call for a chain saw or knowledge of chaos theory, which would both be considered irrequisite variety. They are both tools, but they're superfluous in that context.

Redundancy

- In addition to portfolio effects and requisite variety, a third way in which diversity promotes robustness is redundancy and overlap. For example, government needs checks and balances—such as Congress, political parties, courts, and people—which can all be thought of as diverse tools. Each of these checks can fail, and each works somewhat differently. If one fails, then we can rely on another to correct it. Because each one can fail, it's important that we have others.

- People often fail, and so do the institutions that we construct. Therefore, we may need even more than requisite variety—we may need redundant and overlapping variety. That way, if at first we don't succeed, we can try again. However, rather than trying again in the same way, we can try differently, and in doing so, be even more likely to succeed.

Important Terms

Ashby's law of requisite variety: The claim that the number of responses must equal the number of disturbances.

beta: A statistical measure that equals the normalized covariance between 2 random variables. The beta between random variables a and b equals the covariance of a and b divided by the variance of b.

covariance: A statistical measure that captures whether 2 random variables both tend to be above average at the same time (positive covariance) or if, when one is above its mean, the other tends to be below its mean (negative covariance).

Suggested Reading

Page, *Diversity and Complexity*, chap. 6.

Questions to Consider

1. Why would someone seek negative covariance in his or her investments?

2. What does Ashby's law of requisite variety say about the number of tools that we need as the world becomes more complex?

Inescapable Benefits of Diversity
Lecture 20

O n average, diverse populations should be better, more robust, and more productive. However, in reality, we don't get the average. In this lecture, you will learn how the benefits of diversity are inescapable through the use of 4 examples that involve ecosystems of different levels of diversity. In the first 3 examples, diversity plays no direct role, but in the fourth example, it will be assumed that diversity lowers survivability of the system—and even in this case, diversity appears to have a positive empirical effect. Finally, the diminishing returns diversity theorem puts all of these results within one framework.

Diverse, Moderate, and Homogeneous Ecosystems

- In the following 4 examples, orchards contain diverse types of fruit trees: apple (A), banana (B), cherry (C), and date (D). In the examples, an orchard with 3 trees is an ecosystem, so there are 20 possible ecosystems, and they can be classified as diverse, moderate, and homogeneous. In each of the 4 examples, we will be comparing the average probabilities of survival of each of the 3 classes of ecosystems.

- Diverse ecosystems are those that contain 3 types of trees.
  - ABC ABD ACD BCD

- Moderate ecosystems are those that contain 2 types of trees.
  - ABB AAB AAC ACC
  - AAD ADD BBC BCC
  - BBD BDD CCD CDD

- Homogeneous ecosystems are those that contain 1 type of tree.
  - AAA BBB CCC DDD

Example 1

- In this first example, any ecosystem with an apple tree survives with certainty, and any ecosystem without an apple tree dies with certainty. To calculate the average robustness level for each class, you need only to calculate the percentage of ecosystems within each class that contain an apple tree.

- Of the 4 diverse ecosystems, 3 contain an apple tree, so the average probability of survival equals 75%; 6 of the 12 moderate ecosystems contain an apple tree, so they have an average probability of survival of 50%. Only 1 of the 4 homogeneous ecosystems contains an apple tree. Therefore, they have an average probability of survival of only 25%.

- The diverse ecosystems have the highest average probability of survival. However, diversity per se does not drive survivability—apple trees do. Diversity proves beneficial because more diverse ecosystems are more likely to contain apple trees, a single robust species.

Example 2

- In this second example, survivability again only depends on apple trees, but there are 2 more assumptions. First, the more apple trees in an ecosystem, the more likely the ecosystem survives. Second, the benefits of additional apple trees decrease in the number of apple trees: The first apple tree increases survivability more than the second, and the second apple tree increases survivability more than the third.

- For the purposes of this example, let the probability of survival for an ecosystem with 1, 2, and 3 apple trees equal 60%, 90%, and 100%—respectively. These numerical values capture the 3 core assumptions: that only apple trees matter, that more apple trees are better; and that the added benefit of an additional apple tree decreases in the number of apple trees.

- Among the 4 diverse ecosystems, 3 contain exactly 1 apple tree. Each of those 3 ecosystems has a probability of survival of 60%, and the fourth, BCD—which contains no apple tree—has a probability of survival of 0. Therefore, the average probability of survival equals 45%.

- Of the 12 moderate ecosystems, exactly 50% contain apple trees: 3 contain 2 apple trees, and 3 contain only 1 apple tree. A straightforward calculation gives an average probability of survival of 37.5%.

- Only a single homogeneous ecosystem contains an apple tree, and it has 3, so its probability of survival is 100%. Therefore, the average across all 4 homogeneous ecosystems is 25%.

- On average, the diverse ecosystems perform best once again. This result is obtained even though diverse ecosystems do not, on average, have more apple trees. In addition, as before, the diverse ecosystems are more likely to contain at least 1 apple tree.

- The first apple tree contributes more to performance than either the second or the third. It is not only averaging that is driving the benefit to diversity; **diminishing returns** do as well.

Example 3

- Up to this point, only apple trees have contributed to survivability. In this third example, the following assumptions are made: All 4 types of trees contribute to survivability, and as in example 2, the contribution of additional trees of the same type decrease in the number of trees of that type. For each type of tree, assume a different contribution to survivability for each additional tree. These assumed contributions can be written in the following table.

Survivability Contribution Table

Tree Type	Tree 1	Tree 2	Tree 3
Apple	50	20	10
Banana	30	20	10
Cherry	20	20	10
Date	20	10	10

- Consider the ecosystems BBD, AAA, ABC, and ABD. The first banana tree of BBD contributes 30 to survivability while the second adds 20. To calculate the probability of survival of the ecosystem BBD, these 2 contributions are added to the contribution of the single date tree (20), which gives a total of 70. Using the same logic, the ecosystem AAA has a probability of survival equal to 80, and the ecosystems ABC and ABD have a 100% probability of survival.

- Consider 3 diverse ecosystems: ABC, BBB, and BBC. Calculating their probabilities of survival requires adding 3 numbers from the first column of the contributions table. Calculating the probability of survival for each of the 4 homogeneous ecosystems requires adding across the columns in the contribution table.

- Given the assumption of diminishing contributions, the numbers in the first column are at least as large as the numbers in the second column, which are at least as large as those in the third column. Given that the average values in columns 2 and 3 are less than the average values in column 1, the diverse ecosystems must be more likely to survive than the homogeneous ecosystems.

- Calculating the probability of survival of BBC (moderate ecosystem) entails taking 2 numbers from the first column of the contribution table (for the first banana tree and the single cherry tree) and 1 number from the second column. This same pattern holds when computing the probability of survival for any moderate ecosystem. The final value will be the sum of 2 values from the first column and 1 from the second.

- The moderate ecosystems must be less likely to survive than the diverse ecosystems, which only take numbers from the first column, but more likely to survive than the homogeneous ecosystems, which take numbers from all 3 columns.

- Explicit calculations give the following average survivability values.

	Probabilities of Survival
Diverse	90%
Moderate	77.5%
Homogeneous	57.5%

Diminishing Returns and the Benefits of Diversity

- These 3 examples all fit within a general class of performance functions: For any example within that class, diversity improves performance. Performance need not be survivability of an ecosystem; it could be productivity of an economy or the number of patents introduced by a research laboratory.

- The following 2 assumptions must be stated in order to understand the diminishing returns diversity theorem.
  - Diminishing returns: The contribution to performance of an additional entity of a type strictly decreases in the number of at least 1 type and does not increase for any of other types.
  - Absence of interactions: Total performance equals the sum of the contributions across the types.

- The first assumption implies that the values in the marginal contribution table do not increase along any row. This clearly holds in the third example, and it's true of the first 2 examples as well. In those examples, for all but the apple trees, contributions equal 0. Therefore, the contribution to performance does not increase for those types of trees. For apple trees, the contribution to performance strictly decreases. Therefore, the diminishing returns assumption holds.

- The assumption that system level performance equals the sum of the types of performance is less realistic than the assumption of diminishing returns, which holds true in a variety of situations in the real world. In almost all cases, interactions between diverse types influence performance. That's especially true in complex systems. Nevertheless, the assumption provides an important benchmark. In some cases, interaction effects will improve performance. In other cases, interaction effects will hinder performance. The theorem reveals a general bias toward diversity appearing beneficial.

- The diminishing returns diversity theorem states that, assuming diminishing returns and absence of interactions, collections with more distinct types will have higher average performance. In other words, as long as the types satisfy diminishing returns and there exist no interactions between the types, then more diversity implies better performance. Complex systems contain myriad interactions between diverse types. Some improve outcomes, and some don't.

Example 4

- In this example, assume that each pair of types produces a negative interaction term that hinders performance—yet diversity still proves to be beneficial. This example builds from example 3, but now for each pair of distinct types present in an ecosystem, the probability that the ecosystem survives drops by x%. Diversity is harmful. For this example, assume that the average probabilities for survival for the homogeneous ecosystems are the same as in example 3.

- Given the assumption of the negative interaction between pairs of diverse types, the average probability of survival of the moderate ecosystems decreases by x% because each moderate ecosystem contains 1 pair of distinct types.

- Similarly, each diverse ecosystem contains 3 distinct pairs of species (AB, AC, and BC), so its probability of survival decreases by $3x\%$. Borrowing from example 3, the probabilities of survival can be written as follows.

	Probabilities of Survival
Diverse	$(90 - 3x)\%$
Moderate	$(77.5 - x)\%$
Homogeneous	57.5%

- A quick calculation shows that if x is less than 6.25%, the diverse ecosystems will still be most robust. A similar calculation shows that for the homogeneous ecosystems to be more likely to survive than the diverse ones, the x has to be almost 11%. This example drives home the general point that even with substantial negative interaction effects, diminishing returns will imply that diverse collections perform better.

Conclusions

- The results of the 4 examples do not imply that when confronted with a novel situation, we should always choose diverse collections. If we have enough information to know what drives performance, then we should select the best collection on the basis of that information. However, we may not know a priori which will work best. If we do not, and if we only get one try, then we should probably choose a diverse collection.

- In this lecture, we calculated average values, which is an unsophisticated statistical test that confounds the benefits from diversity and returns to scale. Using proper statistics, we would find no explicit benefit to diversity because we did not include any synergies. The main point of the lecture is that averaging and diminishing returns to type generate a benefit to diversity even without synergies.

- In order for diversity to not be beneficial, the interactions must be negative, as shown in example 4. Averaging and diminishing returns show that as long as the interactions between diverse types don't produce exceptionally large negative interactive effects, then the average performance of diverse collections should perform better than that of either more moderate or homogeneous collections.

- Given that many systems self-assemble through selection, we might expect a tendency toward more synergistic (positive) interactions than antagonistic ones. Therefore, we might expect diversity to be even more beneficial in practice than in these simple examples.

Important Term

diminishing returns: A decrease in the marginal contribution of an additional member of some type.

Suggested Reading

Page, *Diversity and Complexity*, chap. 6.

Questions to Consider

1. How can diversity produce benefits without synergies?

2. Can diversity be beneficial even if the diverse parts create negative interactions?

The Historical Value of Diversity
Lecture 21

I f a society lacks diversity, it will lack the capacity to innovate—it won't grow. Without diversity, the society will become stagnant and vulnerable to collapse. Those 2 lessons follow from the logic and models that you have learned about throughout this course. The lesson that societies need diversity echoes throughout human history. If we look at societies that have collapsed—whether we consider the Romans, the Mayans, the Easter Islanders, or the member states of the former Soviet Union—we learn the same lesson: Societies that lack sufficient diversity fail.

Collapsed Societies
- In his book *Collapse: How Societies Choose to Fail or Succeed*, Jared Diamond tells the stories of 4 collapsed civilizations: the Easter Islanders, who left nearly 1000 carved stone heads called maoi that range in size from 4 to 72 feet; the Anasazi, who lived in the American Southwest; the Mayans from Central America; and a settlement in Greenland that he calls the Vinlanders. Diamond weaves together descriptive accounts of these failed civilizations with a general theoretical model that highlights 5 reasons for failure.
  - Overharvesting of renewable resources: The Vinlanders grazed cattle on marginal land. The Easter Islanders eventually cut down their entire forests. The Vinlanders carved up thick sod to build roofs for their houses and grazed cattle.
  - Climate change: The Vinlanders suffered through a miniature ice age, and the Mayans and Anasazi suffered through years of drought.
  - Fewer friends: By "friends," Diamond is referring to trading partners. When demand for ivory fell, the Vinlanders had little to trade with people from Scandinavia. As a result, their standard of living fell.
  - More enemies: Wars take resources. For societies struggling to make due on marginal land, any demand on labor will contribute to collapse.

Easter Island, famous for its colossal stone statues called maoi, is the location of a pre-European civilization that eventually collapsed.

- o Cultural and institutional failures: The Norse living in Vinland continued to eat a meat-heavy diet as the topsoil slowly eroded. Remains suggest that in the final winter, Vinlanders slaughtered even the youngest calves for food. All the while, they were surrounded by an ocean that had more than an ample supply of fish.

- According to Fisher's theorem, the rate of adaptation scales with the amount of variation. Adaptation requires 2 mechanisms: one to promote diversity and a second to select the better performers among the variants. If a society—such as the Norse on Vinland or the Mayans in Central America—has a strong culture, it may not allow for much variation. Without variation, the society cannot adapt. Often, societies either have to adapt or die, and behavioral variation enables adaptation.

- Even more importantly, a lack of predictive model diversity can create the illusion that the behavioral diversity isn't necessary in the first place. From the diversity prediction theorem, we can come to the conclusion that if everyone thinks the same way, there are only 2 possibilities: either they're all correct, or they're all wrong. If a society is more diverse in members' ideas, they might have a better chance of survival. Homogeneity of thought often leads to collapse.

Why Nations Fail Economically

- Diamond's collapses all involve populations living on marginal land. Cultural blinders that led to overextraction produced failure—but overextraction is not the sole cause of failure. The question of how and why nations fail has received no small amount of attention from historians, economists, political scientists, and anthropologists.

- Joseph Schumpeter, an Austrian economist, described a process that he called creative destruction, in which economies that thrive constantly churn as new technologies replace the old. This innovation drives growth. Societies that don't enable and permit new technologies to enter—societies that don't encourage creative destruction—won't keep pace.

- The creative destruction described by Schumpeter works in spurts. When a new idea or technology emerges, it creates a playground for the mind. New inventions and new technologies by definition are unfinished and unrefined. Early cars, trains, and even computers were relatively primitive. This allowed large numbers of people with lots of diverse ways of thinking to tinker with them and experiment.

- In his book *The Nature of Technology: What It Is and How It Evolves*, economist W. Brian Arthur asks us to think of specific technologies as species that evolve and adapt over time. He then wants us to think of the body of technology in a particular area—the computer industry or kinesiology, for example—as a local ecosystem with many interacting species. Finally, all of technical knowledge can be thought of as analogous to the biosphere.

- Arthur provides elaborate accounts of how new innovations within an industry consist of recombinations of existing parts—just as was discussed in Weitzman's model of growth. Arthur's big idea is that when someone sees a problem, they seek out a solution. Sometimes, a solution will already exist, but other times, a solution won't exist, which results in someone trying to find one. The way that's typically done is through recombination.

- Once we have Arthur's ecosystem metaphor in mind, though, we realize that progress will entail the new technologies replacing old ones. In addition, as we have more and more parts on the table, we have more things to recombine, implying that the rate at which new technologies supplant old technologies may increase. Thus, at the core of creative destruction lie diverse recombinations.

Solow's Growth Model

- One of the more important economic models of the past 1/2 century was developed by Robert Solow. Suppose that each combination of physical capital (machines and the like) and human labor produces outputs. Physical capital outputs can either be consumed or reinvested as more physical capital. In other words, the economy produces outputs, and those outputs can be in the form of consumptive goods or in the form of more machines.

- There are 2 assumptions of this model. The first is that physical capital depreciates. Machines break down, rust, and need repairs. The second assumption is that the returns to more physical capital are increasing but at a diminishing rate. Both assumptions, for the most part, hold up to empirical checks. Machines do wear out, and although machines do allow people to be more productive, doubling the spending on machines typically won't double output.

- One implication of the Solow model is that absent population growth or technological change (Schumpeter's creative destruction), economic growth will stop. Early on, when physical capital is low, the economy will grow—and it will grow at a pretty good clip. However, at some point, as the amount of physical capital grows larger, 2 factors combine to limit growth: The diminishing returns to more capital imply that the increase in output to more capital falls, and the more capital there is, the more capital that depreciates.

- Capital depreciates at a linear rate. This implies that enormous amounts of output must be dedicated to maintaining the status quo. Output has diminishing returns; depreciation has linear returns. If we invest a percentage of our output into capital, then at some point, depreciation will catch up with investment.

- Eventually, the economy will stagnate at a constant level of economic activity—called the technological bliss point. Given an existing set of technologies, we cannot get perpetual growth. All we can do is head toward this bliss point, where we'll be stuck forever.

- In other words, Schumpeter had it right: Continued growth requires innovation. We cannot just keep pumping money into existing technologies and expect continued growth. Solow's simple mathematics showed that to be impossible.

- Solow's model does a nice job of explaining the rise and fall of the former Soviet states. From 1920 to 1980, the Soviet Union exhibited fantastic growth. By some accounts, its growth rates exceeded those of the United States. Then, suddenly—or so it seems—the Soviet Union dissolved.

- In their book *Why Nations Fail: The Origins of Power, Prosperity, and Poverty*, economist Daron Acemoglu and political scientist James Robinson relate the details of the collapse of the Soviet Union in great detail. They also tell the stories of the Mayans and the Romans. The 3 histories share similar features.

- Schumpeter's historical studies suggested to him that periods of growth exhibited creative destruction. They did, and they continue to do so. The Solow model tells us that absent creative destruction, growth stops. We reach a technological bliss point, and there's no growth beyond that. Add in creeping corruption, and you end up with something worse than stagnation—failure.

- Acemoglu and Robinson, after taking a Schumpeterian-like sweeping view of history and analyzing it with tools like Solow's, agree that we need creative destruction for growth but believe that we also need inclusive political institutions—those that have strong central power and are pluralistic—for creative destruction. They show that the reason that so many countries in Africa and the Middle East have lagged behind other countries is not cultural or based on geography as some others suggest; instead, it's because their political institutions have not created incentives for diverse and deep ways of thinking.

- Countries that are captured by an elite will tend not to allow the creative destruction necessary for growth. For example, during the first decade of the 21st century, the newspaper industry in the United States lost more than a quarter of a million jobs. The growth of the Internet contributed mightily to this demise because people had an alternative outlet for news. However, what hurt the newspaper industry the most may have been a company called Craigslist, which allowed people to place classified ads for free, because revenue from classified ads kept newspapers afloat.

- Without a doubt, Craigslist represents an enormous improvement over the classified ad, but it was a creative destroyer. It was a new product, but it destroyed many more jobs in the newspaper industry than jobs it created. It has clearly made the world a better place—despite all those lost jobs in the newspaper industry.

- Suppose that we didn't have a relatively open society and that we were ruled by an elite. That elite might own the newspapers. In owning those newspapers, it would have every incentive to prevent Craigslist from coming into being. By requiring that all classified ads be posted in newspapers, the government could guarantee an informed citizenry that helps maintain the "healthy democracy." That sort of logic, along with a few fistfuls of dollars, can stall innovation and make entire countries fail.

- In his book *The Collapse of Complex Societies*, Joseph Tainter tells another theory as to why countries collapse. He argues that over time, societies become too complex and that they must devote an increasing number of resources to cope with that complexity. Tainter argues that as we invest in ever more social complexity, we suffer from ever greater increasing returns. We get spread too thin, and we collapse.

- Tainter shows us another place where diversity can be harmful. We don't want our set of problems to be too diverse. If they are, then by Ashby's law of requisite variety, we have to be incredibly diverse to handle them all. That would be fine if these problems were all productive—if solving each problem increased productivity—but it won't. Many of the problems are administrative and suck energy from the system, leading to collapse.

Suggested Reading

Acemoglu and Robinson, *Why Nations Fail*.

Arthur, *The Nature of Technology*.

Diamond, *Collapse*.

Page, "Are We Collapsing?"

Questions to Consider

1. Why does the standard growth model imply a need for constant innovation?

2. Why did Jared Diamond say that societies collapse?

Homophily, Incentives, and Groupthink
Lecture 22

If diversity of thought is beneficial, then the opposite of diversity, groupthink, must not be beneficial. In this lecture, you will be formally introduced to groupthink and why it is dangerous—namely, that it leads to bad outcomes and a lack of adaptability. Then, you will be introduced to conformity, drift, homophily, and incentives, which are all causes of groupthink. In each case, groupthink emerges even though nobody wants it to. You will also learn how to avoid groupthink both as an individual who wants to stand out from the crowd and as an organization that wants to be innovative.

What Is Groupthink?

- **Groupthink** refers to everyone in a community having the same model of how some part of the world works—in other words, everyone thinking the same way.

- In some instances, groupthink can be good. Groupthink is great if what we all think is correct. If there's a chance that we're wrong, however, then it's better if we allow for a little heterogeneity of thought.

- Groupthink can also be good if the people involved are carrying out a common plan. In battle, on a football field, or in a dance performance, you may want everyone following the same script, but in many other contexts, groupthink is bad. It is especially bad when the associated system is in flux.

Football games and dance performances are just a few examples of instances in which groupthink can be good.

- According to Fisher's theorem, the speed of variation depends on the amount of variation. If the landscape dances, then our ability to adapt will depend on how much variation we have. If we all think the same way, there's no variation on which selection can operate. In other words, we're stuck.

- The diversity prediction theorem, which we applied to predictive contexts, states that crowd error = average error − diversity. Groupthink implies that there's no diversity, which means that the only way that the crowd can be accurate is if every member of the crowd is correct. It's clear from the formula that we don't want groupthink—unless we are all correct.

Conformity

- One reason that groupthink comes about is that people often conform to match the behavior and thinking of the majority. We go with the flow for a host of reasons, including feeling insecure.

- Conformity is a powerful thing. In a famous set of experiments, psychologist Solomon Asch showed just how susceptible we are to peer pressure. In this experiment, people were first shown a card with a line of a particular length. They were then shown the card with segments A, B, and C and were asked to pick the segment that most closely matched the first line segment.

- In the experiment, there were a group of confederates and one person being tested. Asch ran 18 trials. In 12 of the 18 trials, the confederates all gave the wrong answer. In those cases, approximately 1/3 of the students gave the wrong answer as well. In other words, they conformed. Even more amazingly, 75% of people conformed to the incorrect majority at least once.

Drift

- Drift is the second cause of groupthink, and it is more subtle. To demonstrate how drift can create groupthink, let's construct a simple model. Suppose that you are part of a 10-person management team. Suppose that there are 2 equally compelling ways to look at the actions of a competing firm: You could think that firm is trying to maximize market share or trying to be the low-cost provider.

- For the purposes of this example, suppose that the truth is some combination of those 2 and that as long as people in your firm think both motivations are in play, you'll be able to predict the competitor's actions with some degree of accuracy. In other words, you would like to preserve diversity.

- Each person on the management team has 1 of those 2 ideas in his or her head. The people that think that the competitor cares only about market shares will be denoted by Ms, and the people that think that the competitor cares about costs will be denoted by Cs. In this model, the management team can be represented by a set of 10 letters—some are Ms, and the rest are Cs.

- Suppose that when 2 people meet, one of them, with some probability, changes his or her opinion to match that of the person he or she is talking with.

- This differs from conformity because under conformity, everyone would change their minds to match the majority view. Under drift, people match the model, or type, of another person without taking into account the frequency of that type. They just copy; they don't move to the majority.

- Here are the rules for the model.
    - Rule 1: Randomly pick an influencer.
    - Rule 2: Randomly pick an influencee—someone who will change his or her opinion.
    - Rule 3: Change the type of the influencee to match that of the influencer.

- Suppose that there are 5 Ms and 5Cs. To get 1 more M, you would have to pick an M first (probability = 5/10) and then pick a C (probability = 5/9). Therefore, with a probability of 25/90, or 5/18, there will be 1 more M. By the same logic, with a probability of 5/18, there will be 1 more C. That leaves a probability of 8/18 that even numbers of Ms and Cs are maintained. Note that it is just as likely to go up 1 as down 1.

- Next, suppose that there are 8 Ms and 2 Cs. To get 1 more M, you would have to first pick an M (probability = 8/10) and then a C (probability = 2/9), which leads to a total probability of 16/90. The odds of picking a C first equal 2/10, and the odds of picking an M second equal 8/9. Again, this leads to a probability of 16/90. Therefore, it is just as likely to go up as down. That's why this phenomenon is called drift.

- You might also notice that this effect moves a little more slowly when it reaches an extreme. At 50/50, there is a 25 out of 90 chance of going up. At 80/20, the odds fall to 16/90. That's because it becomes less likely to get a pairing of 2 people with different opinions when one opinion occurs more often than the other.

- If you run this model for a while, you will find that the system bounces around; formally, it's considered a random walk, but eventually it will end up at all Ms or all Cs. Once either of those points is reached, there's no more drift. Mathematicians call these absorbing states; we call them groupthink.

- This is a simple model. Suppose that you construct a more elaborate model with thousands of people and dozens of opinions. You will still end up with drift, and that drift will eventually depress diversity. If you let the drift occur for long enough, a single opinion will dominate, and you'll have groupthink.

- If we combine these first 2 models—conformity plus drift—people would tend toward the majority but could occasionally move in the opposite direction. When we combine the models, we're likely to see a little less groupthink than the conformity model would suggest and a lot more than we'd expect from pure drift. What's important is that we're still going to see groupthink.

Homophily

- Our third cause of groupthink is called **homophily**, which combines the Greek roots for "same" and "love." In other words, we like to hang out with people who are like us—or at least who we think are like us. Research shows that people sort by race, income, political views, and even types of movies.

- Homophily produces groupthink at the local level because we only interact with people like us, so we never encounter any diversity. This explains why everyone in a firm can think the same wrong thing or why sometimes groups of people do offensive things.

- Although homophily creates groupthink at the local level, it can maintain diversity at the global level. In fact, it almost guarantees it. That doesn't mean homophily is a good thing, however. If the diverse groups don't interact, you just have 2 groups of groupthinkers that are each failing in their own way.

- When you see people hanging out who look, act, and think similarly to one another, you might wonder whether it stems from conformity, drift, or homophily. Social scientists call this the identification problem. Unless you have temporal data that would help you see people move and change, it's almost impossible to tell. You cannot tell if they're hanging out together because they're similar or if they're similar because they are hanging out together.

Incentives

- The last cause of groupthink is incentives. If we all have incentives to perform best as individuals, we likely will choose the same models to carry around in our heads.

- It might seem strange, but in fact, your organization, firm, or family may often be better off if you think in the second best way. It could be that your colleague is right more often than you are, but that doesn't mean that you should necessarily change how you think. Collectively, you'll be better off if you continue to refine your different, less accurate model than to copy some other person's better model.

- Sticking to your guns, therefore, is one way to avoid groupthink. Groupthink can not only lead to individually bad decisions, but it can also lead to systemic collapse.

Avoiding Groupthink

- The first 2 causes of groupthink—conformity and drift—can be avoided in several ways. First, you can restrict communication by putting in fire walls. It's hard to mimic people if you don't know what they're doing. Once you allow communication, you open the door to groupthink.

- However, putting in a fire wall comes at a cost: We lose the ability to recombine ideas and models—a huge benefit of diversity. We have no hope of getting better solutions through deliberation or recombination.

- Therefore it's often preferable to make people leap before they look. In other words, require that people first write down how they think and then have a discussion. In this case, people can be free to change their minds and conform later, but at least their ideas get out there.

- Another way to avoid conformity is to create a culture in which people challenge rather than acquiesce. The idea of constructive conflict is that it has to be okay to disagree; otherwise, people will mimic.

- A final way to prevent mimicry—another type of fire wall—is to create greenfields, which involves taking a group of people and putting them in a separate location (greenfield) so that they're not influenced by the same sets of ideas.

- For the most part, we overcome drift in much the same way that we overcome conformity. By limiting communication, leaping before you look, creating a culture of constructive conflict, and using greenfields.

- Drift can also be slowed by changing social networks. If some people have high charisma or many contacts, they may speed the process of drift. If you can get rid of these super spreaders, you can reduce drift.

- Another way to prevent drift is to encourage people to mutate not copy. For example, suppose that someone recommends a book to you on Roosevelt by Edmund Morris. A natural reaction would be to read the same book—but that's drift in action. Instead, you might think about reading a biography and perhaps read one about Lincoln, Tubman, or Jackson. This prevents drift and injects diversity.

- Even though we cannot necessarily distinguish homophily from mimicry, the methods to combat it differ. One method is to mix people up. Some companies randomly reassign offices; others make sure that people switch positions or locations with some regularity.

groupthink: The tendency for a group of people to think about a problem or situation in the same way.

homophily: When people choose to interact with people who are similar to themselves.

Suggested Reading

Page, *The Difference*, epilogue.

Questions to Consider

1. How do we connect the concept of groupthink to the diversity prediction theorem?

2. What are the causes of groupthink?

The Problem of Diverse Preferences
Lecture 23

U p until this lecture, you have learned about how diversity improves such areas as prediction, problem solving, and robustness, but in this lecture, you will confront the inconvenient fact that a different type of diversity—preference diversity—creates problems. Preference diversity creates cycles, and the presence of cycles means that people have incentives to misrepresent their true preferences. In addition, in the context of problem solving, people can expend a lot of energy trying to come up with better solutions but end up running in circles. Finally, if different actors with diverse preference can be gate keepers, then policy improvements may be thwarted.

What Is Preference Diversity?

- Preference diversity (wanting different outcomes) differs from cognitive diversity (possessing different ways of thinking). Cognitive diversity solves problems, but preference diversity creates them.

- Social scientists represent preferences in 2 ways. When we're talking about preferences for a particular quantity, we will often try to write a functional form. If different people have different preferences, then they have different functions and, therefore, different graphs. The functional form approach works best when we're only considering 1 or 2 dimensions—such as time spent swimming, percentage of income spent on housing, or hours of leisure.

- The functional form approach won't work very well if we're considering discrete, multidimensional things, such as houses or advertising plans. In those cases, social scientists rely on preference orderings, which are listings of the possibilities in order of how much they are liked. For any 3 options, for example, if you prefer option A to B and B to C, then you can write your preference orderings as A > B > C. If someone else prefers B to C to A, then you can write his or her preference orderings as B > C > A.

- Diverse preferences won't matter if we're making individual choices, but when groups of people must make collective decisions or have to solve a problem together, then preference diversity can create enormous problems.

Arrow's Impossibility Theorem

- Arrow's impossibility theorem, which was proposed by economist Kenneth Arrow, states that if we have diverse preferences, then there's no way for us to aggregate them in all cases into a general, collective ordering.

- For example, suppose that 3 friends are trying to decide where to go to dinner and can choose from an Italian, a Mexican, and a Chinese restaurant. Abby likes Italian best, then Chinese, and then Mexican. Bethany likes Chinese best, then Mexican, and then Italian. Callie prefers Mexican, then Italian, and then Chinese.

- The preferences for these 3 friends can be written as follows.
  o Abby: Italian > Chinese > Mexican.
  o Bethany: Chinese > Mexican > Italian.
  o Callie: Mexican > Italian > Chinese.

- Notice that each person has rational preferences, which means that the alternatives can be ordered. Irrational preferences would mean that someone likes Italian more than Chinese and Chinese more than Mexican, but he or she likes Mexican more than Italian. That would be crazy—or what social scientists call "irrational."

- In this example, it will turn out that even though each person is rational, as a collective, the group is irrational. If the group votes on Italian versus Mexican, then Mexican wins because Bethany and Callie both prefer Mexican. If the group then votes on Chinese versus Italian, Italian wins because Abby and Callie both prefer Italian. Finally, if they vote on Mexican versus Chinese, Chinese wins because Abby and Bethany both prefer Chinese to Mexican.

- The collective preferences are Mexican > Italian > Chinese > Mexican. In other words, the group likes Mexican more than Italian and Italian more than Chinese and Chinese more than Mexican, which in turn they like more than Italian. The group has what is called a preference **cycle**. It's similar to the simple hand game rock-paper-scissors: Rock beats scissors, scissors cut paper, and paper covers rock.

- This shows that if people have diverse preferences, then they might have some trouble using voting to come up with the best alternative because it won't work. Arrow's impossibility theorem says something even deeper—that nothing will work other than a dictator. This means that if people use any procedure for coming up with a collective ranking, they'll always get cycles—unless that procedure is to let someone be a dictator.

- In the formal mathematical version, Arrow's theorem requires some assumptions. For example, if we add some new possibility and the rankings of 2 alternatives don't change, then the theorem requires that their final ranking doesn't change.

- If people have different preferences, then it will be really difficult to come up with a ranking of the alternatives. In other words, each member of a group can have rational preferences, but if the individuals are diverse, then the group may not have rational preferences. The group may be irrational.

The Gibbard-Satterthwaite Theorem

- Arrow's theorem hints at a second result—that it might make sense to be strategic. If what happens through some voting process will be arbitrary, perhaps the process can be manipulated to get what you want.

- In the previous example, suppose that the 3 people decide that they are first going to vote on Chinese versus Italian, and then the winner will run off against Mexican. If everyone votes truthfully, then Italian will win the first round because both Abby and Callie vote for it. However, then Mexican will win the second round. Unfortunately, Mexican is Abby's least favorite choice, so she's not going to be happy.

- To get what she wants, Abby could misrepresent her preferences in the first round and say that she likes Chinese more than Italian. If she does, then Chinese would win both rounds, and she would get to eat Chinese. You might consider this to be lying, but game theorists call this strategic voting.

- Allan Gibbard and Mark Satterthwaite proved that any voting system that isn't a dictator can be manipulated by strategic voting.

- Kenneth Arrow proved that there is no good way to aggregate diverse preferences, and Gibbard and Satterthwaite proved that whatever method we use (which, according to Arrow, will be flawed) is subject to manipulation. These theorems imply that if the members of a group have diverse preferences, the group's preferences may be ill defined and, therefore, people might lie.

Preference Diversity and Problem Solving

- Suppose that a company designs tablet computers and that these tablets have 3 relevant attributes: pixels, speed, and memory. In addition, suppose that there are 3 people working on design teams to come up with a new version of the company's tablet computer: Andrea, Brian, and Carlos.

- Andrea cares about pixels and speed—but not at all about memory. Brian cares about memory and speed but doesn't think that the number of pixels matters very much. Finally, Carlos cares about memory and pixels but not speed. Hence, the 3 designers all have different preferences.

- Suppose that Andrea introduces a laptop called the Alpha that has 60 pixels per square centimeter, a processing speed of 50 megahertz, and a memory of 32 gigabytes.

- Assume that each person gives a score to each tablet using the following rules.

Tablet 1: 60 pixels, 50 megahertz, 32 gigabytes

Name	Rules	Score
Andrea	Pixels + Speed	110
Brian	Memory + Speed	82
Carlos	Memory + Pixels	92

- Notice that Brian likes tablet 1 less than the others, so he works on a new design. He applies some new heuristics for how to get more memory and speed out of the tablet, and after substantial work, he proposes a new design called the Beta.

Tablet 2: 50 pixels, 70 megahertz, 24 gigabytes

Name	Rules	Score
Andrea	Pixels + Speed	120
Brian	Memory + Speed	94
Carlos	Memory + Pixels	74

- Suppose that we now take a vote, and tablet 2 wins by a vote of 2 to 1. Therefore, it seems like the better tablet. However, Carlos isn't happy because he thinks that the new design has insufficient pixels and memory. Then, he works tirelessly to build a tablet that he likes better—called Gamma.

Tablet 3: 40 pixels, 60 megahertz, 48 gigabytes

Name	Rules	Score
Andrea	Pixels + Speed	100
Brian	Memory + Speed	108
Carlos	Memory + Pixels	88

- Once again, the firm is divided, so they hold a vote. Notice that the Gamma defeats the Beta because both Brian and Carlos prefer it. However, then Andrea is not happy; the Gamma is her least favorite tablet of the 3. She liked the original tablet best, so she proposes a vote on the Alpha against the Gamma. Andrea prefers the Alpha and, it turns out, so does Carlos. Notice that we have a cycle. The Beta defeats the Alpha and the Gamma defeats the Beta, but the Alpha defeats the Gamma.

- In the case of the 3 friends picking a restaurant, these voting cycles created problems because the group wouldn't be rational, and there were incentives for people to misrepresent what they want.

- In this context, however, we're talking about problem solving, and the cycle arises when people try to find better solutions. The result becomes not continuous improvement but running around in circles—going from one table to the next.

- If people disagree on which direction is up, there can be a lot of misplaced effort. As a result, enormous effort can be spent getting nowhere. Brian and Carlos did a lot of work, but it had no positive effect. In that case, preference diversity is not helpful.

- These observations about diverse preferences can partly explain why governments often aren't as productive as we might hope. For example, the members of the United States Congress have talent and a high level of diversity of perspectives and heuristics, but they also have different preferences. Democrats and republicans want different things, and they represent people from different states and districts who may also want different things.

- The problems may be even worse than just cycles. Given that the 2 parties often share power, one party may hold the White House and another may hold one or both houses of Congress. This, in effect, gives both parties veto power, implying that only bills that both parties believe to be improvements will become policy. This problem of veto players has been studied in depth by political scientist George Tsebelis.

- To see why multiple veto players with different preferences cause problems, suppose that any policy has 2 dimensions: an efficiency dimension and an equity dimension. Suppose that Republicans care only about efficiency and that Democrats care only about equity. The average voter might care about the 2 dimensions of a policy equally.

- The problem is that someone could propose a policy that the average voter likes more than the status quo, but it could fail to pass. In addition, because policies are less likely to pass, members have less incentive to spend time trying to come up with new policies—thus, magnifying the first effect.

Important Term

cycle: A situation in which outcome a is preferred to b and b is preferred to c, but c is preferred to a.

Page, *The Difference*, chap. 9.

Questions to Consider

1. What is a preference cycle?

2. What does the Gibbard-Satterthwaite theorem say about honesty in politics?

The Team. The Team. The Team.
Lecture 24

I n the previous lecture, you were left with the question of how to cope with preference diversity, and to some extent, there's a one-word answer: leadership. Great leaders get everyone on the same page. They also get people to recognize the distinction between fundamental preferences—what we really want—and instrumental preferences—the policies and actions we take to achieve our fundamental preferences. To instill the total commitment required for the success of the University of Michigan's football team, former coach Bo Schembechler was famous for saying "The team. The team. The team." And he is not alone in making that exhortation.

What You Know

- If we're trying to make a choice that will lead to good outcomes, diverse categorizations, interpretations, and mental models lead to diverse predictions, which lead to better collective outcomes. However, diverse preferences over outcomes (which would seem to result from diverse models) cannot be aggregated without cycles, and outcomes can be manipulated by acting strategically. In other words, we want diversity in how we think but not diversity in what we want.

- Fundamental preferences are what you really want; they are your preferences over outcomes. Perhaps you want good health, economic security, and happy times with your family and friends. For your organization, you may want to build good products, offer valuable services, and increase market share.

- Fundamental preferences are contrasted with instrumental preferences, which are your preferences over the instruments or policies that produce the outcomes over which your fundamental preferences are defined. If 2 people have different instrumental preferences, then they differ on which of 2 actions would help them better achieve their fundamental goals.

- Diverse fundamental preferences mean that someone is going to be unhappy, and as in the case of choosing a place to eat, that person might have an incentive to misrepresent his or her preferences. In fact, the Gibbard-Satterthwaite theorem tells us that someone will.

- Diverse fundamental preferences are bad. However, diverse instrumental preferences are good. They imply diverse predictive models for how to get good outcomes. We can use these to come up with good collective predictions and, as a result, to take actions that enable us to get good outcomes, given our fundamental preferences.

The Phillips Experiments

- For their experiments, Katherine Phillips—along with Katie Liljenquist and Margaret Neale—recruited a group of volunteers from 2 fraternities or sororities. In this way, everyone had the same gender to get any gender bias out of the way. People were then presented with a murder-mystery task and were asked to solve it. This is a predictive task.

- The researchers formed groups of 3 people from the same fraternity who all had the same prediction and let them talk. For some groups, they added a fourth person from the same fraternity who shared their opinion. For the other groups, they added someone from the other fraternity who had the different opinion.

- The first team is homogeneous in 2 ways: They hang out together, and they think alike. The second team differs in 2 ways: They don't hang out together, and they also think differently from one another.

- The researchers then let these groups interact and make predictions, and they found that the more diverse group made more accurate predictions. On predictive tasks, we should expect the more diverse group to predict more accurately.

- The researchers also asked people how effective they thought their group was. People thought that the homogeneous groups were more effective, and they were also more confident in their decisions because no one was disagreeing with them. When people disagree with you, it can be less fun, and it can make you less confident.

- Thus, experience and reality may not line up. Good experience (everyone agrees) could lead to a bad reality (not a good decision), and bad experience (people disagree) could lead to a good reality (an accurate prediction).

Tying Everything Together

- In reality, you go to a meeting and people disagree. You have to ask yourself: Is this fundamental disagreement or instrumental disagreement? If it's the former, then you have to push for pulling back on the reins and stopping the wagons. No organization, group, school, or even family will be able to consistently make good decisions if you don't agree on your fundamental objectives. This is where leadership enters.

- Great leaders do 2 things. They get people to agree on fundamental preferences. Without those, cycles and manipulative behavior can result. Leaders also get people to agree on the goal. Leaders do not necessarily get people to agree on how to achieve that goal—at least not initially.

- For any decisions that you make, sometimes you'll be on the winning side, and sometimes you'll be on the losing side. However, this winning and losing is only with respect to instrumental choices; it's not true with respect to fundamental outcomes. In fact, all that you learned earlier in this course tells you that you should be happy when the group disagrees about instrumental choices, but that's just difficult to accept sometimes.

- In the Phillips experiments, the task was assigned. The goal was to predict accurately. Therefore, we can say with almost certainty that any disagreement was instrumental and not fundamental, which was why the diverse groups did better.

- If you go to a meeting and there's disagreement, what should you think? If the disagreement stems from diverse fundamental preferences, that's a bad thing. If it stems from diverse instrumental preferences, then the diversity was probably a good thing.

- Suppose, though, that you go to a meeting and everyone agrees. You might think that you are lucky to have a fun, smart team, and much like the people in the Phillips experiments, you might be really happy. However, if you all agreed, it must be true that there was no diversity. Either there was no cognitive diversity in the room (which is bad), or the problem was so easy that you all saw the same correct solution. In the latter case, you should correctly infer that unless you like meetings, you probably just lost an hour of your life that you'll never get back.

- The logic we've just walked through explains why companies such as Hewlett-Packard promote both common goals and diverse ways of solving problems. When companies such as Hewlett-Packard promote diversity, they mean cognitive diversity. They want to tap into diverse perspectives, diverse categorizations, diverse models, and diverse heuristics without worrying about diverse preferences getting in the way.

- If you go to a meeting and everyone agrees, it's probably not a very good meeting in terms of making a good decision—although it might have been a great meeting in terms of building morale. However, if you go to a meeting and people disagree, if you find that your models—not you, but your ways of thinking—get challenged, and if you're pretty sure those challenges stemmed from instrumental and not fundamental preference diversity, then you should be happy.

- If you want to be a good leader, you have to enforce the logic of the team and get everyone on the same page with respect to fundamental preferences. Then, you also have to create an inclusive culture in which people can share their diverse ways of thinking.

Lessons Learned

- W. Brian Arthur, who wrote about the nature of technology, believes that in an economy, the problem of problems (what problems do we want to solve?) drives innovation. He argues that advances come about because someone sees a problem and wants to fix it. In order to fix it, the person looks around at all the diverse technologies that exist and sees if he or she can find some way to recombine them to fix the problem. This isn't always the case. Sometimes solutions go in search of problems. In other words, the problem that was solved may not have been recognized until someone had a solution to it.

- Mostly, though, the places we go depend upon where we would like to go—and what we're capable of doing. Progress depends on identifying problems and then putting together diverse minds to solve them.

- In their book *Why Not?: How to Use Everyday Ingenuity to Solve Problems Big and Small*, Ian Ayres and Barry Nalebuff describe many instances of someone seeing a problem, fixing it, and gaining the economic spoils.

- We all see problems. We see places where we can make the world better, and we set out to try to do just that. If this is true, then preference diversity has an upside. It leads us to pursue diverse ventures. If we care about different things, then we see different problems and opportunities, and this leads to all kinds of wonderful ideas, forms of artistic expression, and products. Furthermore, all of these things can be combined. Sometimes, when one of us solves a problem in our own interest, we also solve a problem or create an opportunity for others.

- The tools that a person has—including his or her perspectives and heuristics—will be influenced by his or her preferences. What we care about plays an enormous role in what we learn and study and, therefore, in how we see the world.

- Perhaps diverse preferences aren't so bad after all; they provide fuel for the diverse cognitive skills that drive collective performance. However, if within an organization, such as our government, we have preference diversity, then we might find ourselves running around in circles. Alternatively, if our institution creates multiple veto players, then we may be handcuffed in what we can achieve because we have to satisfy too many people.

- Organizations can avoid this problem by agreeing on a common goal. However, that doesn't mean that it's easy to keep everyone on the same page. Good managers go to great lengths to keep people on task. Unfortunately, the government has no such luxury. The government has to make policies for all of us, and we all have to deal with them.

- In their book *The Priority of Democracy: Political Consequences of Pragmatism*, political theorists James Johnson and Jack Knight demonstrate that the success of a political system depends in large part on how well formal and informal institutional arrangements overcome the problems created by that diversity. Acemoglu and Robinson, who wrote about why nations succeed and fail, would add that a political system's success also depends on how well it frees up and taps into the cognitive diversity of its people.

- Within teams and organizations, a common objective enables more efficient leveraging of cognitive diversity. Lack of a common objective is similar to having a really lousy oracle—one that only tells you the truth some percentage of the time. Lack of a common objective will make finding better solutions difficult.

- That doesn't mean that we don't want some preference diversity. Preference diversity leads us to identify different problems. This may help us to prevent collapse, and the solutions to those problems can improve our lives and can be repurposed to solve other problems.

- As for politics, we just have to hope that we can all get along and perhaps compromise a little more. If we can, the big team—the team of all of us—will lead more fulfilling, interesting lives. As members of that team, we have to ask ourselves: What tools should I acquire? What challenges and opportunities should I identify as my own? The answer to those questions won't stay fixed; they will adapt.

- To thrive and contribute as individuals, we need to acquire depth and sophistication, and we need to accumulate new perspectives and new heuristics—or else we as individuals may collapse. Collectively, we need even greater diversity. We need to maintain that diversity in the face of our natural tendency to conform and in the face of the loss due to drift and incentives—which requires that we encourage people to think differently.

Suggested Reading

Page, *The Difference*, chap. 10.

Questions to Consider

1. Why might preference diversity be such a bad thing after all?

2. Why do leaders focus so much on the team having a common goal?

Glossary

adaption: A change in behavior or actions in response to a payoff or fitness function.

Ashby's law of requisite variety: The claim that the number of responses must equal the number of disturbances.

bell curve: A normal curve, or distribution.

beta: A statistical measure that equals the normalized covariance between 2 random variables. The beta between random variables a and b equals the covariance of a and b divided by the variance of b.

category: A collection of similar events or objects.

cognitive diversity: Differences in the perspectives, heuristics, and categories that an individual uses to make predictions and find solutions to problems.

complex: A term used to describe a system that is between ordered and random and is difficult to explain, evolve, or predict.

covariance: A statistical measure that captures whether 2 random variables both tend to be above average at the same time (positive covariance) or if, when one is above its mean, the other tends to be below its mean (negative covariance).

crowdsourcing: Using large numbers of people to find a solution to a problem—usually done over the Internet.

cycle: A situation in which outcome a is preferred to b and b is preferred to c, but c is preferred to a.

dancing landscape: A fitness or payoff landscape that is coupled so that when one entity changes its action, it causes the other entity's landscape to shift.

diminishing returns: A decrease in the marginal contribution of an additional member of some type.

diversity: Differences in types of entities.

diversity prediction theorem: The collective error for a crowd equals the average error minus the diversity of the predictions.

diversity trumps ability theorem: In problem solving, groups of diverse problem solvers can outperform groups consisting of the best individuals.

global optimum: The best solution to a problem.

groupthink: The tendency for a group of people to think about a problem or situation in the same way.

heuristic: A technique or rule for finding improvements in the current best solution to a problem.

homophily: When people choose to interact with people who are similar to themselves.

local optimum: A peak on a rugged landscape.

interdependence: The influence of one entity's action on the behavior, payoff, or fitness of another entity.

network: A collection of nodes and links, or connections between the nodes.

no free lunch theorem: Any 2 heuristics that test the same number of points have the same expected value across all possible problems.

normal distribution: The distribution that results from averaging random shocks of finite variance.

perspective: A representation of the set of possible solutions to a problem.

recombination: The combining of existing ideas and technologies to create new ideas and technologies.

robustness: The ability of a complex system to maintain functionality given a disturbance or internal dynamics.

rugged landscape: A graphical representation of a difficult problem in which the value of a potential solution is represented as an elevation.

simulated annealing: A search algorithm in which the probability of making an error decreases over time.

Six Sigma: Refers to the region within 6 standard deviations of the mean.

specialization: The practice of having individuals perform a single task so that they can improve at that task.

standard deviation: The square root of the variance of a random variable. In a normal distribution, 68% of all outcomes lie within 1 standard deviation.

theory of comparative advantage: A theory that shows how 2 countries can both benefit from trade, provided each is relatively better at producing some good.

variance: Differences in the value of an attribute (informal). The expected value of the squared error of a random variable (formal).

Bibliography

Acemoglu, Daron, and James Robinson. *Why Nations Fail: The Origins of Power, Prosperity, and Poverty.* New York: Crown Books, 2012.

Arthur, Brian. *The Nature of Technology: What It Is and How It Evolves.* New York: The Free Press, 2009.

Bell, Robert M., Yehuda Koren, and Chris Volinsky. "All Together Now: A Perspective on the Netflix Prize." *Chance* 23, no. 1 (2010): 24.

Diamond, Jared. *Collapse: How Societies Choose to Fail or Succeed.* New York: Viking Press, 2005.

Florida, Richard. *The Rise of the Creative Class: And How It's Transforming Work, Leisure, Community, and Everyday Life.* New York: Basic Books, 2002.

Gould, Stephen Jay. *The Mismeasure of Man.* New York: W. W. Norton, 1996.

Hong, Lu, and Scott E Page. "Groups of Diverse Problem Solvers Can Outperform Groups of High-Ability Problem Solvers." *Proceedings of the National Academy of Sciences* 101, no. 46 (2004): 16385–16389.

———. "Problem Solving by Heterogeneous Agents." *Journal of Economic Theory* 97 (2001): 123–163.

Howe, Jeff. *Why the Power of the Crowd Is Driving the Future of Business.* New York: Crown Publishing, 2008.

Lamberson, P. J., and Scott E. Page. "Optimal Forecasting Groups." *Management Science* 58, no. 4 (April 2012): 805–810.

Lemann, Nicholas. *The Big Test: The Secret History of the American Meritocracy*. New York: Farrar, Straus, and Giroux, 1999.

Mokyr, Joel. *The Gifts of Athena: Historical Origins of the Knowledge Economy*. Princeton, NJ: Princeton University Press, 2004.

Page, Scott E. "Are We Collapsing? A Review of Jared Diamond's *Collapse: How Societies Choose to Fail or Succeed.*" *Journal of Economic Literature* 43, no. 4 (2005): 1049–1062.

———. *Diversity and Complexity*. Princeton, NJ: Princeton University Press, 2010.

———. *The Difference: How the Power of Diversity Creates Better Groups, Firms, Schools, and Societies*. Princeton, NJ: Princeton University Press, 2007.

Pande, Peter, Robert Neuman, and Roland Cavanagh. *The Six Sigma Way: How GE, Motorola, and Other Top Companies Are Honing Their Performance*. New York: McGraw-Hill, 2000.

Suroweicki, James. *The Wisdom of Crowds*. New York: Anchor Books, 2005.

Tetlock, Phil. *Expert Political Judgment: How Good Is It? How Can We Know?* Princeton, NJ: Princeton University Press, 2005.

Weitzman, Martin L. "Recombinant Growth." *Quarterly Journal of Economics* 113, no. 2 (1998): 331–360.

Wolpert, David H., and William G. Macready. "No Free Lunch Theorems for Optimization." *IEEE Transactions on Evolutionary Computation* 1, no. 1 (April 1997): 67–82.

Notes

Notes

Notes

Notes

Notes

Notes